# SOLD OUT
## LIVE FOR JESUS

## CARLA MCDOUGAL

LUCIDBOOKS

# Foreword by Scot Pollok

I have a strong opinion about the current state of the church here in the west. I've seen the rapidly changing culture around us have its ever present influence on the family of Christ's church. We are distracted and filled with fear. Our most foundational convictions about God and truth are being incessantly questioned and attacked. Our connectivity has dissolved into a pasty thin veneer of something we label "community" but is far from it. A deep anger and frustration exists just under the surface of almost everything around us, such that the tiniest prick in the right spot and it violently erupts. What is happening? How is the church of God responding? How is the body of Christ being influenced? What difference are we making for the Kingdom of God?

Without wanting to be a dark cloud or a killjoy, the unexpected truth is that these words could have been easily written at the time of the Apostle Paul. They would have been as accurate then as now.

Perhaps this is why books like the one you hold in your hand from Carla McDougal are so important. *Sold Out* is anchored in one of the greatest written statements we have from Paul. He wrote it to the infant church in the backwoods town of Philippi. He penned it in prison. The joy he expressed in this central statement and those that come before it speak to an unusual joy.

*My dear friends*, Paul says in my paraphrase, *we are bonded together as a family because of Jesus. And I want you to know that just because I'm in prison, the power of the Gospel has not been shackled. I shared Jesus Christ with lots of the prison guards. They have believed and in turn shared it with others. The motives are diverse but I rejoice because Jesus is being shared no matter what. Yes, I am so very happy because no matter if I live or die, Jesus Christ is being celebrated and trusted.*

Then it hits. In Paul's own words, *"for to me, to live is Christ and to die is gain."* Philippians 1:21

He says *this is why I live. To spur others to trust and celebrate Jesus is my whole life! If I physically perish in this joyful adventure, it is only a good thing because I'll be with Him perfectly.*

The power of this statement has inspired countless men and women on to maturity, to mission, to martyrdom. It has been an anchor for the church throughout two millennia of shifting sands and seasons. It remains worthy of careful study, seasoned meditation and intentional practice.

What Carla does in this very accessible journey is to employ a thoughtful trajectory at a very lofty goal: to make Paul's statement a livable reality today. With helpful tools in each section designed to contextualize application and inspire habits of personal engagement with God's Word, Sold Out works like a tuning kit for your heart. Carla is not only one of the most joyful and spirited intercessors and teachers in our church family, she has worked very hard to encourage you with her latest labor of love. I sincerely pray it blesses you richly.

Scot Pollok
Lead Pastor, Faith Bible Church
The Woodlands, Texas

# DEDICATION & ACKNOWLEDGMENTS

*S*old Out is dedicated to the readers of my book, *My Prayer Chair—A living, walking, breathing relationship with Jesus.* While *My Prayer Chair* focuses on developing inward conversations with God, *Sold Out* encourages us to live for Jesus every day through our actions, thoughts, and conversations. *Sold Out* continues the prayer journey.

\*\*\*

I thank all of you who read *My Prayer Chair.* Your encouragement, prayers, and words of affirmation inspired me to write *Sold Out: Live for Jesus.*

A huge love-hug goes to my husband and best friend, Fred. "Thank you for your prayers along the way. You always spur me forward to accomplish God's purposes. I love you."

To my dear friend, Kitty Self… "Thank you for helping me to express my creative ideas with clarity and understanding. Your gift as an editor and teacher blesses me beyond words. Wow, just thinking about the laughter we shared throughout the writing and editing process creates a big smile all over my face! And yes, we are still having fun."

To my daughter-in-law, Brianne McDougal, "Thank you

for saying yes to being on the cover of *Sold Out*. I love you dearly!"

Jake Allen, "Thank you for developing the *Sold Out* cover. It is perfect!"

Looking to use *Sold Out* as a Bible study
for a small group?

Download the free *Sold Out Leader's Guide* (PDF) at:
www.reflectivelifeministries.org

# TABLE OF CONTENTS

# SOLD OUT
# LIVE FOR JESUS

*For to me, to live is Christ and to die is gain.*
— Philippians 1:21

Live. Breathe. Exist. Time seems to move so quickly. But why? Is the clock revolving faster and faster? Do blocks of time vanish as if they never existed? Are we so focused on ourselves that one day fades into the next? Do we live only to exist?

God desires for us, as believers in Jesus, to live every day in victory—not for ourselves, but for Him. From the moment we wake up, God waits for us to connect with Him. He looks forward to a time of sweet communion with His children.

God's tender voice calls, but do we listen?

The more we focus on Jesus, the more we recognize the sound of His voice. Asking God to help us live every moment through Him and on His time schedule changes our perspectives and purposes in life. The result—we become more Christ-centered and less self-centered.

*Sold Out* is based on Paul's statement in Philippians 1:21, *For to me, to live is Christ and to die is gain.* In other words, life is not about me, but all about Jesus. From a prison cell, Paul wrote in Romans 14:7-8, *For none of us lives for ourselves alone and none of us dies for ourselves alone. If we live, we live for the Lord; and if we die, we die for the Lord. So, whether we live or die, we belong to the Lord.*

To understand the fullness of these verses, we must grasp what the word *live* actually means. The original definition comes from the Greek word *zao*, which means to be fresh, strong, and effective.[1] The phrase *to be* calls us to aggressively pursue a relationship with Christ— twenty-four hours a day, seven days a week. This quest strengthens and refreshes our relationships with Him and allows us to affect His Kingdom.

*Sold Out* encourages you to draw nearer to Jesus. It inspires you to live for Him through your actions, words, and thoughts, changing your focus from yourself to Jesus. Watch for opportunities to practice His biblical principles and ask God to help you live every day sold out for Jesus.

# CHAPTER 1

# REFRESH YOUR CONNECTIONS

*I appeal to you, brothers, in the name of our Lord Jesus Christ, that all of you agree with one another so that there may be no divisions among you and that you may be perfectly united in mind and thought.*

—1 Corinthians 1:10

U nity. Harmony. Oneness. Over and over in God's Word, He commands His children to stay connected. He calls us to function as the body of Christ, working together to affect His Kingdom. In the book of Mark, Jesus issues a mandate to all believers...

*He said to them, "Go into all the world and preach the good news to all creation. Whoever believes and is baptized will be saved, but whoever does not believe will be condemned."*
—Mark 16:15-16

Jesus charges us with spreading the message of salvation and redemption to the nations. In Matthew 28:19, God instructs His children to...

*Go and make disciples of all nations, baptizing them in the name of the Father, the Son, and the Holy Spirit.*

By God's design, He allows His children to be His hands, feet, and voice here on earth. The Father of the entire universe, Maker of heaven and earth, King of kings and Lord of lords allows His children to be a part of His Kingdom work. Engulfed with humbleness, I surrender, sold out to Jesus.

God gives believers individual assignments. Thankfully, the moment we trust in Jesus, He sends His Spirit, the Holy Spirit, to indwell us. As we seek the Lord, the Holy Spirit reveals God's purposes for us to accomplish. When God's children operate in their spiritual gifts, the body of Christ functions properly. Overall, God's plan makes perfect sense. However...

Satan and his demons wait for just the right time to attack believers in Jesus. His goal is to bring disunity within the body of Christ and tear our relationships apart. Why? Not because he can have us, but because he wants to halt us from furthering and affecting God's Kingdom. When believers connect and work together, it brings strength to our families, churches, friendships, ministries, and to all areas of our lives. Jesus is the victor forever and ever. Amen.

So, does unity contain the power to strengthen the whole? Absolutely! Let this chapter encourage you to seek God-given connections in and through your life. Ask the Lord to open your eyes to...

- His tender voice.
- Spiritual puzzles in your lives.
- Daily divine assignments.
- Spiritual planting techniques.
- His daily protection.

Live sold out for Jesus in every relationship. Pray for unity. Ask for godly wisdom and understanding.

# ~GOD HEARS~
# PRAY 911

*He who dwells in the shelter of the Most High will rest in the shadow of the Almighty.*

—Psalm 91:1

Turmoil surged. Tears poured. Confusion erupted. Negative thoughts bombarded my mind. I felt like I was in a war zone. Dropping to the floor, I cried out for God's strength and protection from this oppression...

*God, there is no way I can speak at this women's retreat! I am too weak. How can you use me if I feel this way? I just want to crawl into a hole.*

Suddenly, Psalm 91:1 popped into my head, *He who dwells in the shelter of the Most High will rest in the shadow of the Almighty.* Opening my Bible, I decided to read all of Psalm 91. In seconds, I found myself praising God for allowing me to suffer through this mental chaos and utter confusion. My weakness opened the door to a fresh experience with Jesus. That evening, as I walked onto the stage, the Holy Spirit strengthened me from head to toe *in the shadow of the Almighty.* The Lord God receives all of the glory!

The next day, I shared my experience with one of my close friends. With a gentle answer, she said, "Carla, when this happens to you, call or text me so I can pray for you!" I told her I didn't realize what was happening at the time, but agreed to call or text her if it happened again.

This conversation lingered in my mind. Later that evening, I read Psalm 91 again. I focused on Psalm 91:1 and to my surprise this is what I saw—911. My heart pounded with excitement! Thoughts ignited. *The next time I experience one of these spiritual warfare attacks, I need to text - PRAY 911 - to my prayer team!* I jumped up and started praising God for how He works in and through our situations.

## LIFE CHALLENGE

I challenge you to use this same method. Ask God to raise an emergency prayer team, so that in the midst of a difficult situation, circumstance, or spiritual attack, you can text—PRAY 911. They don't have to know the details. God knows them. Through prayer, He gives us the opportunity to participate in eternity here on earth. Standing in the gap for one another is a two-way blessing. Share this new idea with others. As God leads you to form or join a PRAY 911 team, don't hesitate to live sold out for Him as you pray for others.

## PRAYER JOURNAL

Read Psalm 91. Write out the verse or verses that touch your heart. Ask God to reveal why this section speaks to you. Call out to Him to help you put this verse to action and live for Him.

# ~GOD DESIGNS~ HIS KINGDOM PUZZLE

*From Him the whole body, joined and held together by every supporting ligament, grows and builds itself up in love, as each part does its work.*

—Ephesians 4:16

Round puzzles. Square puzzles. Jigsaw puzzles. Crossword puzzles. Heart puzzles.

All have one thing in common — the pieces fit together to complete the whole. When one segment is missing, the full picture is distorted.

Just as a missing link weakens the chain, an omitted puzzle piece alters the final image.

A few years ago, we purchased a small shed for our trash containers. The box included the instructions and all of the unassembled parts. Assembling the shed reminded me of putting together a puzzle. After the shed was constructed, to our surprise, one piece was left over, leaving the shed unstable and wobbly. Reading back over the instructions, we discovered that we skipped one of the steps, which affected the outcome. It was crucial to backtrack and insert the leftover piece. In the end, the shed was sturdy and useable.

This real life puzzle-building analogy reminds me of the Christian life. Think of the body of Christ as the unassembled pieces in the box and the instructions as God's Word to His children. When we fail to follow God's instructions, we easily end up like our first attempt in building the shed — unstable and wobbly in our walk with Christ. However, when we follow His guidelines, the result is a steady and strong relationship with Jesus.

Let's do a simple comparison of assembling the shed to the Christian life...

- THE FORCED PIECE—Sometimes we try to fit ourselves into ministry positions that God planned for someone else in His Kingdom puzzle. We don't allow God to fit us where He wants us. The result—confusion rather than peace.

- THE MISPLACED PIECE—Sometimes we, as the connected pieces, try to fit others into ministry positions rather than allowing God to create and finish His Kingdom puzzle. The result—disunity rather than harmony.

- THE TAKEOVER—The shed required assembling all the pieces together in their specific places for the end product to be strong and useful. Likewise, God's Kingdom puzzle is made up of all believers in Jesus. When one tries to fit into too many places, the puzzle is weakened. One person cannot do it all. For example, a ministry leader who fails to delegate misses the blessings of working together as a team. The result—exhaustion and frustration rather than strength.

God created us to work together as the body of Christ, beautifully designed to accomplish His purposes. God's Kingdom puzzles are best created by Him, for Him. His beautiful mosaics form an exquisite panorama of His Glory.

## LIFE CHALLENGE

Within His Kingdom puzzle, do you love others unconditionally, with all your heart, soul, mind, and strength? Do you find yourself trying to fit where God hasn't really placed you? Are you trying to force others into ministry positions? Ask God to show you His plan and purpose for you as you serve Him. Remember, He is the ultimate puzzle builder. His designs bring perfection and completion. When we work within God's guidelines, His Kingdom is strengthened. This spurs us forward to live every day sold out for Jesus.

## PRAYER JOURNAL

Read Ephesians 4:1-16 with 1 Corinthians 12:12-31 and 1 Corinthians 13. Absorb God's Word. Note: 1 Corinthians 12:12-31, which focuses on unity, precedes 1 Corinthians 13, known to many as *The Love Chapter*. Hmm... it seems as if God is telling us something very important. Journal your thoughts.

# ~GOD APPOINTS~
# DIVINE
# ASSIGNMENTS

*Paul and his companions traveled throughout the region of Phrygia and Galatia, having been kept by the Holy Spirit from preaching the Word in the province of Asia. When they came to the border of Mysia, they tried to enter Bithynia, but the Spirit of Jesus would not allow them to. So they passed by Mysia and went down to Troas.*

—Acts 16:6-7

My seat assignment—17A. The last row in the airplane. Immediately, negative thoughts rushed in... *I won't be able to recline my seat. I have to listen to the engine roar the whole way home. I'll be the last one off the plane!* But my spirit quickened after the Lord reminded me of my prayer that morning: "Lord, please give me a divine seat assignment on the airplane. Amen." I stopped grumbling and anticipated His appointment.

Right before the passengers started boarding the plane, my husband was called to the boarding counter. He was offered an upgrade to first class because of his airline status. After receiving it, he calmly turned and handed it to me saying, "I want you to have this seat." With a willing heart and a sigh of relief, I said, "Oh, you are so sweet. YES, I'll take it!" Looking at the ticket, I noticed the seat assignment was now 1C. *Woohoo!* I thought to myself.

I secured my items and made myself comfortable in my newly assigned seat. At the same time, the lady next to me arranged her belongings. Now sitting side-by-side, a conversation sparked. You know the surface talk... Do you live in Houston? Where do you work? How often do you travel out of town? After takeoff, our conversation deepened. She asked me about my occupation. I replied with the usual, "I'm a Christian author and speaker." Immediately, the Holy Spirit reminded me of my morning prayer, "Lord, please give me a divine seat assignment on the airplane."

In a matter of minutes, the woman opened up and poured out her story to me. Before I knew it, we were praying together. I shared how my originally assigned seat was on the last row of the plane, but God shuffled the seats around to place me on the first row. In tears, she grabbed my hand and we thanked God for allowing us to sit next to each other. We still stay in touch through email. I praise God for how He orchestrated a divine assignment.

Sometimes unexpected changes or circumstances might actually be divine appointments. Focusing on God changes our perspective. Realizing we, as God's children, are His hands and feet helps us keep a heavenly point of view, resulting in a life sold out for Jesus.


## LIFE CHALLENGE

Ask God for a divine assignment today. Ask the Holy Spirit to help you recognize it and follow through with all God has planned. It is so much fun serving our Lord and Savior, Jesus. What a blessing to take part in a divine appointment. Again, I am reminded, "It's not about me, but all about Him!" Live sold out for Him through your daily activities, conversations, and prayers. Look for ways God opens doors for His children to connect and unite as one.


## PRAYER JOURNAL

Read Acts 15:36-41 and Acts 16:1-15. Notice all of the divine assignments along the way. Praise God for the appointments He has planned for you today.

# ~GOD PLANTS~
# HIS GARDEN

*I planted the seed, Apollos watered it, but God made it grow.
So neither he who plants nor he who waters is anything, but
only God, who makes things grow. The man who plants and the
man who waters have one purpose, and each will be rewarded
according to his own labor. For we are God's fellow workers,
you are God's field, God's building.*

—1 Corinthians 3:6-9

One spring, we experienced a heavy amount of rain, which led to a greater than normal weed population. I frequently armed myself with gardening gloves, old shoes, sunscreen, and determination to rid my flowerbeds of these unwanted plants.

One day, as I raged war in the front flowerbed, I noticed a plant that looked different from the others. *What is this growing in the flowerbed? I pulled weeds for hours a few days ago and now look—another weed emerges its ugly head.* But its broad leaves and vibrant color caused me to hesitate. After careful examination and an Internet search, I realized a watermelon seed rooted itself near the front entrance of our house. I immediately showed it to my daughter, Carly Jo. She begged and pleaded with me to not pull the plant. I gave into her excitement and granted the little plant a reprieve.

I must be honest. I just knew this vine was not going to produce a watermelon. First of all, we didn't plant the seed. Plus, we were leaving to go on vacation for two weeks. But to my surprise, while we were gone, the vine tripled in size! And to top it off, a baby watermelon protruded from the vine as if to say, "Thank you for allowing me to grow in your front yard."

My heart pounded with excitement as I showed Carly Jo the growing fruit. The joy of her enthusiasm blessed me beyond words. Wrapping her arms around me, she exclaimed, "Thank you for not pulling up the plant when you first discovered it growing in the flowerbed!"

I have no idea how the watermelon seed embedded itself in the flowerbed. Possibly someone spit out a seed while eating some fruit. Over time, the seed was covered with dirt and sprinkled with water. In God's perfect timing, the seed germinated, roots formed, and the watermelon appeared.

## LIFE CHALLENGE

It's interesting how God teaches life lessons through real life experiences. As believers, we never know the spiritual seeds we spit out as we go through our day. The more we live sold out for Jesus, the easier it is to talk about Him as we walk along the way. In God's perfect timing, He covers those spiritual seeds with His love, grace, and mercy. He then allows others to come along to water the seeds with words of affirmation and encouragement. Still others nourish the soil with nutrients from God's Word and through prayer. Just like the roots of a plant, spiritual roots must establish themselves before growth occurs. In time, as the spiritual vine strengthens, fruit begins to appear. God has spiritual lessons ready and ripe for the picking in His perfect timing. You never know what seeds are taking root before your eyes.

## PRAYER JOURNAL

Read 1 Corinthians 3. What verses capture your attention? Write them out. What is God teaching you?

# ~GOD PLANS~
# NO EXPECTATIONS

*For He will command His angels concerning you, to guard you in all your ways.*

*—Psalm 91:11*

A mazed. Grateful. Overwhelmed. Still in awe of God's constant presence. Tears of joy and thankfulness wrap a bow around my heart. Let me explain...

Our journey started on Tuesday, September 30, 2014. Four Texas friends flew to the Newark Airport, just outside of New York City. I met Rhonda, Cheryl, and Lisa at the car rental office. We decided that we needed a big vehicle to accommodate our four extremely LARGE suitcases— Texas women don't travel lightly. We packed up the SUV, settled into our seats, and headed out for the adventure of a lifetime.

Faith Baptist Church in Rexford, New York, booked me as the speaker for their annual women's retreat. My friends decided to come along with me for a fun girl's trip. We needed to be at Camp of the Woods in the Adirondack Mountains by Friday, so this left us three days to meander our way through upstate New York.

We titled our trip *No Expectations*. I served as the chauffeur, a scary thought for some of you. Rhonda held the position of co-pilot. We called her the map-a-gator. Cheryl and Lisa supplied encouragement from the backseat. We started with a prayer, asking God to protect us, direct our path, and to show us His glory.

Each curve in the road presented a fresh portrait of God's beauty. Like feathers falling from the sky, the autumn leaves gracefully swirled in the air before blanketing the hills and valleys. Experiencing this seasonal change created a sweet peace along with unforgettable memories.

For three days, we followed the GPS (God's Positional System, as we called it) up to Cooperstown, over to Saratoga Springs, finally ending at Camp of the Woods Retreat Center near Speculator, New York. God provided divine appointments all along the way. We prayed with a couple who stayed in our same bed and breakfast, prayed with sales clerks, gave food to the homeless, engaged in Jesus conversations with strangers, and so much more. All the while, we continued praying for the upcoming retreat.

We reached our destination on Friday, and excitement escalated as sixty-five women greeted us with hugs and big smiles. Our theme for the weekend—*Operation Basic Training: Equipping Yourself for the Battle.* Each session focused on the enemy's tactics for the battles we face in our minds, thoughts, emotions, and relationships. God moved powerfully during the retreat. Our final group prayer time amazed and overwhelmed us all.

Throughout the weekend, I urged the ladies to prepare for the next week. Why? Because many times, God gives us opportunities to practice what He teaches us through His Word. I encouraged them to ask the Lord to reveal ways He spiritually goes to battle for their lives. And I reminded them to never forget to praise Him before they know the answers to their prayers. One of our focus verses was 2 Chronicles 20:15, *Do not be afraid or discouraged because of this vast army. For the battle is not yours, but God's.* Little did I know, God was preparing our Texas team for what was coming.

The retreat closed around 4 p.m. on Saturday. After packing the car and saying our goodbyes, we started our four-hour road trip back to a hotel near the Newark Liberty Airport. A drizzling mist set the scene for our journey. I must say, we were extremely tired, yet completely energized. Streams of praises flowed as we reflected on the retreat, the divine conversations, the prayer time, and more. Joy filled the car. Until...

BOOM! BAM! BANG! Like the sound and jolt of an explosion, our car vibrated and bounced around. Screams erupted. Lisa cried out from the back seat, "Something is wrong! Seriously, something's not right!"

My thoughts began to spiral... *We must find a place to pull over. God make a way for us!*

Lisa again echoed in her sweet, yet serious tone, "Something is wrong! Something's not right! Something is between my feet!"

Cheryl reached down to feel the floorboard. "Oh, my! There's something down here." Using her phone, she turned on the light for a closer look. "Oh, no! A piece of metal is coming through the floorboard! I can feel the air coming through the hole!"

Rhonda burst into prayer, "God, help us!" As she prayed, we passed a vehicle going about thirty miles an hour. This seemed odd, but we didn't realize the significance until later.

The car was driving fine, but there was no safe place to

pull off the road. We drove another fifteen, fear-filled miles until we could stop. All four of us jumped out of the car and bent down to take a look. In unison, we shouted, "It's a muffler!"

We tried to dislodge it ourselves, but it wouldn't budge. We asked a man to help us remove the part from under the car. He couldn't believe his eyes! After thanking him for his assistance, we got back into the car. Paralyzed and stunned, we tried to figure out how that piece of metal wedged itself under the car. Our conversation moved from "This kind of thing just doesn't happen" to "God sent His angels to watch over us."

We discussed the event over and over. We concluded that the muffler broke loose from the slowly moving car. The impact of the fall obviously changed the shape of the front of the muffler to look more like an arrow or missile. As we talked, the what if's started pouring out. *What if...* it shot into a tire? *What if...* it penetrated the gas tank? *What if...* it went through the brake line?

Reality surfaced. *What if...* the whole muffler made its way through the car? At that moment, our jaws dropped, and our bodies weakened.

The muffler lodged itself right between Lisa's feet. One inch to the right or left, and it would have sliced through her foot. The piece of metal was angled straight for Lisa's body.

Even now, writing this causes my heart to quicken and thankfulness to pour over me. No doubt—God appointed

His angels to watch over us. No doubt—God's angels guided this evil arrow to lodge itself in the perfect position to cause the least amount of damage. God reminded us of Psalm 91:11... *For He will command his angels concerning you, to guard you in all your ways.*

Together, we praised the Lord for His provision, protection, love, grace, and mercy! We thanked all of the people who prayed for us on our New York journey... family, friends, the Reflective Life Ministries' Prayer Team, and all of the ladies from the Faith Baptist Women's Retreat.

On another note, thankfully, I purchased the Damage and Collision Insurance. The rental car employee said in all her years she'd never seen anything like this. Honestly, this near accident paved the way for a great opportunity to share about God's grace, mercy, and love through Jesus.

In summary, our *No Expectations* prayer at the beginning of the trip was answered above and beyond what we could imagine. God directed our path, showed us His glory, and appointed His angels over our trip.

## LIFE CHALLENGE

Imagine this scene: You're driving down life's highway when out of nowhere something shakes your world. An unexpected jolt ignites fear, anxiety, and panic. You have a choice—to zero in on the incident or see beyond it. Choosing to focus on the incident only leads to confusion and worry. Looking beyond the obvious allows you to see God in the midst of the trouble. Ask God to help you view your circumstances through His eyes. Thank Him for His protection along the way. You never know when God's angels will show up... *For He will command His angels concerning you, in all your ways.* AMEN.

## PRAYER JOURNAL
Read Psalm 34. Write out the verse that touches your heart. Write out a testimony of God's protection over your life. Praise Him.

# CHAPTER 2
# REFUEL YOUR HEART

*Love the Lord your God with all your **heart** and with all your
soul and with all your mind and with all your strength.*
— Mark 12:30

W hat does it mean to love the Lord with all your heart? Are humans capable of loving this way? In this verse, the meaning for heart comes from the Greek word, *kardia*, which focuses on the heart being the seat of all spiritual and physical life.[2]

Just as blood continually refuels our physical heart, Jesus, through the Holy Spirit, refuels the spiritual heart. Spending time in God's Word and praying throughout the day fuels us with His love, grace, and mercy.

Before you read the entries in Refuel the Heart, pray for the Holy Spirit to reveal truth to you. Look for these main points in this chapter...

- As believers in Jesus, we are forgiven—past, present, future.
- God promises to never leave us or forsake us.
- God, through Jesus, through the Holy Spirit, reveals how to pray.
- God's Word connects our hearts to His.
- A grateful heart creates a thankful attitude, which refuels the heart.

Be prepared to experience sweet moments with your Savior, Jesus. Be inspired. Be encouraged. Be ready. May each entry in this chapter ignite a fire in your heart to live sold out for Jesus.

# ~FORGIVENESS~
# FRESH START

*If anyone is in Christ, he is a new creation; the old has gone, the new has come.*

—2 Corinthians 5:17

Fresh start. New beginnings. Forgetting what is behind and pressing forward. What does this really mean: *The old has gone, the new has come?*

For some, it means a new commitment, like a New Year's Resolution—regular exercise, eating healthy, following a daily routine, changing an attitude, using self-discipline, modifying an old habit, or reading through the Bible in a year. But is there more to it than just making physical life changes? Absolutely. Digging into God's Word, the Bible, gives us a greater understanding of God's Truths. Let's examine Philippians 3:12-14.

*Not that I have already obtained all this, or have already been made perfect, but I press on to take hold of that for which Christ Jesus took hold of me. Brothers, I do not consider myself yet to have taken hold of it. But one thing I do: Forgetting what is behind and straining toward what is ahead, I press on toward the goal to win the prize for which God has called me heavenward in Christ Jesus.*

Paul is writing to the church in Philippi, to believers in Jesus. Paul is not talking about working his way to a position in heaven. He secured this spot the minute He trusted in Jesus. Paul focuses here on the condition of His relationship with Jesus and becoming more like Him every day.

Paul is clear to point out that his past sins would always be before him. But he refused to let them dictate who he was in Christ. Prior to Paul's face-to-face encounter with Jesus in Acts 9, his job was to arrest followers of the Way—followers of Jesus Christ. More than likely, etched in his memory were the innocent Christians he witnessed being stoned, imprisoned, persecuted, and even beaten to the point of death. But because of Jesus' forgiveness, Paul was freed from his past. Every day, Paul chose to live in victory, not in defeat because of his former life.

What a beautiful picture of God's love, grace, and mercy! Paul encourages us, as we mature as Christians, to press forward in living sold out for Him. We are forgiven—past, present, and future. Filled with hearts of forgiveness, we are new creations in Christ. The old has gone. The new has come. Don't allow the enemy to throw the guilt of the past onto you. Leave it at the foot of the cross. Jesus paid it all. A fresh start awaits you each day. Rest in Him.

## LIFE CHALLENGE

Do you live in defeat? Does guilt invade your heart and mind, or do you press forward accomplishing God's purposes in your life? Begin by asking God to give you a heart of forgiveness for yourself as well as others. It is vital to trust and believe what Paul proclaims... *the old has gone, the new has come.* The moment you said "yes" to a relationship with Jesus, He sent His Spirit, the Holy Spirit, to live inside of you. The Spirit sealed the deal with a mark that says, "This one is Mine!" As a believer, you can never be snatched out of His hand. Now, you are equipped to live sold out for Jesus. Believe it. Know it. Live it.

## PRAYER JOURNAL

Read 2 Corinthians 5:14-21 with Philippians 1:21. Write out the verse that impacts your heart. Journal your prayers, confessions, and petitions.

# ~UNDERSTANDING~
# NEVER FORSAKEN

*My purpose is that they may be encouraged in heart and united in love, so that they may have the full riches of complete understanding, in order that they may know the mystery of God, namely, Christ in whom are hidden all the treasures of wisdom and knowledge.*

—Colossians 2:2-3

Bewildered. Puzzled. Confused. This mystery remains unsolved in our home.

As a mother and wife, I perform my weekly household duties. But, I must confess, the chore I dread the most is the laundry. Mainly it's because of, what I call, The Single Sock Mystery.

For over thirty years of marriage, I've tried to solve this sock dilemma. Maybe between the washing and drying procedures the socks reproduce? Possibly a sock snatcher lives in the dryer. Does anyone else have this problem? I'd really like to solve this mystery!

One summer, we housed some college students working as interns at our church. This brought the number of people living under our roof to seven. Occasionally, our clothes mixed together, which caused a great deal of confusion. One night, I folded a few loads of laundry and ended up with a record—eighteen mismatched socks. Without thinking, I shouted, "I don't get it! Why does this happen over and over? How do I end up with so many single socks?"

As usual, I added them to the other singles collected over the years. My hope was that one day they would find a match and live happily ever after. Suddenly, this thought surfaced… *I am so thankful God doesn't stick me in a drawer when life doesn't make sense. When things seem mismatched and out of sorts, the Lord doesn't toss me aside in hopes I will find my own answers. God promises never to leave me or forsake me.*

Immediately, God reminded me of Colossians 2:2-3…

*My purpose is that they may be encouraged in heart and united in love, so that they may have the full riches of complete understanding, in order that they may know the mystery of God, namely, Christ in whom are hidden all the treasures of wisdom and knowledge.*

Praises released, peace surfaced, and thankfulness resounded. As I prayed, I sensed God saying, "Carla, My daughter, open your eyes and heart to My spiritual life lessons throughout the day. They teach you My truths and help you experience My grace, love, and mercy." A tender love message straight from God to my heart— forever remembered, never forgotten.

## LIFE CHALLENGE

Are you confused about a situation? Do circumstances in your life not make sense? Do you feel like a mismatched sock shoved in a dark place? Please read Colossians 2:2-3 one more time. I love how Paul says... *My purpose is that they may be encouraged in heart.* Be encouraged, my friend. Jesus loves you and will never forsake you. Ask God to give you a heart of understanding. He is there twenty-four hours, seven days a week, to lift you from the dark places in life. Call on Him. Trust Him. Surrender it all to Jesus.

## PRAYER JOURNAL

Read Colossians 3:1-17. Write out the verse that stands out to you. Journal your thoughts.

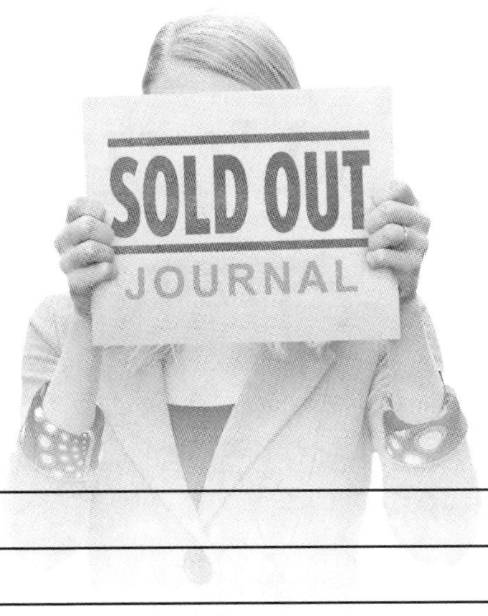
SOLD OUT
JOURNAL

# ~PRAYER~
# GOD'S ULTIMATE
# PLAN

*But when He, the Spirit of truth, comes, He will guide you into all truth. He will not speak on His own; He will speak only what He hears, and He will tell you what is yet to come. He will*

*bring glory to Me by taking from what is Mine, and making it known to you. All that belongs to the Father is Mine. That is why I said the Spirit will take from what is Mine and make it known to you.*

—John 16:13-15

Have you ever wondered, "Do I pray to God the Father or Jesus the Son? Does it really matter? What is the meaning of prayer?"

First and foremost, we must understand and grasp that God exists in three distinct persons who are the same in nature, but distinct in function: the Father, the Son, and the Holy Spirit. Diving into scripture opens the door to understanding. God reveals His mysteries through His Word. Reading through John 16:13-15, Jesus unlocks the "Who do I pray to" mystery through His conversation with His disciples.

Visuals help us understand biblical concepts. Think of how a clock operates. It continuously moves in a right-to-left forward direction. Look at the My Prayer Clock image.

Here is my explanation of the prayer connection...

Jesus had to go away so the Holy Spirit could come to the disciples and ultimately to us. Everything that belongs to God also belongs to Jesus. God makes all things known to Jesus. In turn, Jesus passes everything on to the Holy Spirit. Then the Holy Spirit reveals everything to us. The

Holy Spirit never speaks on His own. He only affirms what Jesus makes known to Him.

Just as the clock is in continuous motion, so is the work of God the Father—through Jesus—through the Holy Spirit. The more we listen, the more we understand how to specifically pray for circumstances, family, friends, acquaintances, world situations, government leaders, ministry opportunities, and more. According to God's ultimate prayer plan, when we talk to God, we pray back to Him what He has already made known through Jesus to the Holy Spirit. Before we know it, we are living, walking, and breathing moment-by-moment conversations with God.

Keep in mind, communicating with God includes listening as well as talking. Developing ongoing, prayerful conversations with Him takes practice. Begin by talking to Him about your daily thoughts, actions, and needs. Take it all to Him. Nothing is too small or too big for God to handle. He gives us the privilege to participate in eternity here on earth through prayer. (For more on prayer, read Carla McDougal's book *My Prayer Chair.*)

## LIFE CHALLENGE

Practice using the Prayer Clock analogy. Remember, God's ultimate prayer plan begins with God the Father, revealing through Jesus and then through the Holy Spirit, how and what to pray. Ask God for spiritual insights and directions. Then listen to the Holy Spirit as He directs your prayers. Ask God to give you a heart of prayer. Be prepared for some exciting revelations as you dive into a deeper, more intimate prayer life.

## PRAYER JOURNAL
Read John 16:1-16. Write down the verse that touches your heart. Journal your prayer.

# ~GOD'S WORD~
# SCRIPTURE HUNT

*Love the Lord your God with all your heart and with all your soul and with all your strength. These commandments that I give you today are to be upon your hearts. Impress them on your children. Talk about them when you sit at home and when you walk along the road, when you lie down and when you get up. Tie them as symbols on your hands and bind them on your foreheads. Write them on the doorframes of your houses and on your gates.*

—Deuteronomy 6:5-9

Young. Married. Graduate school. Just enough money to make it through each month. I worked full-time while my husband, Fred, labored diligently to complete his graduate degree while working as a professor's assistant. Despite our meager income, our relationship strengthened. Just the two of us, satisfied and secure.

From the beginning of our marriage, we set our life plan—or so we thought. After graduation, our goal was to find a job, build a savings account, and start a family.

But hidden deep within my heart was the desire to be a mother. I continued asking God to remove this yearning during this time of our lives. To suppress it. To hide it. To cover it. Still, the passion for being a mom burned. God knew my heart, and He was in control. I prayed for the day when I would hold my baby for the first time.

Then, the unexpected happened.

Scared, yet excited.
Fearful, yet trusting.
Scattered, yet collected.

*How are we going to make it? Fred is still in graduate school. Oh, God, this wasn't the plan!*

After nine months of pregnancy, anxiety surged. *Lord, fear is setting in. My thoughts rage out of control. Please show us how to raise our child to know and love You.*

Suddenly, an idea popped into my mind. Grabbing my Bible, I started a scripture hunt. With the turn of every page, I prayed for God to show me a verse to pray over my baby. Then it happened. Deuteronomy 6:5 seemed to leap off the page. *You shall love the Lord your God with all your heart, with all your soul, and with all your strength.* My heart pounded. Praises lifted. Blessings flowed.

Overcome with humbleness, I thought of Fred. *He loves You, God, with all His heart, soul, mind, and strength.* Tears welled up. *Thank you, God, for my husband, our marriage, our baby, and showing me this life verse.*

The time arrived and two became three.

I loved watching our baby boy sleep. Words couldn't express my unconditional love for him. I started praying Deuteronomy 6:5 over him—*Lord, help Luke love you with all his heart and all his soul and all his strength.* Joy resonated in my heart. A memory forever embedded in my soul.

Through the years, God blessed us with two more boys and a precious daughter. This verse continues to serve as the life verse for my husband, myself, and all of my children. I thank God for the way He directed me to His Word. He receives the glory and honor forever and ever. Amen.


## LIFE CHALLENGE

God's Word refuels our spiritual lives. The Bible is our guide on how to live a life sold out for Jesus. The more we center on scripture, the more we know Jesus and how to live for Him. Ask God to show you a focus verse for your life, relationships, circumstances, or possibly for the year. Pray before you begin the scripture hunt. If you are married, ask the Lord to reveal a focus verse for your marriage. If you struggle with family issues, ask God to reveal a scripture for your relationships. And if you have children or grandchildren, ask Him to give you a verse to pray over them. Relish the moments in His Word through this scripture hunt. Take to heart all God is doing in your life. Reading His Word leads to living His Word, which inspires a life sold out for Jesus.

## PRAYER JOURNAL

Read Deuteronomy 6. Write out Deuteronomy 6:5 and Luke 10:27. Journal your thoughts and prayers.

# ~Praise~
# Thankful Heart

*Enter His gates with thanksgiving and His courts with praise; give thanks to Him and praise His name. For the Lord is good and His love endures forever, His faithfulness continues through all generations.*

—Psalm 100:4-5

You need to be thankful for what you have. Please change your attitude. Thankfulness creates humbleness.

Do these phrases ring a bell? I remember my mom using them on a regular basis. Her way of discipline was not only through words, but also through facial expressions. As a child, when I displayed an ungrateful attitude, my mom could speak without saying a word. Do you know what I mean? My sisters and I called it—The Look. Every time the look targeted one of us, it was our clue to straighten up and act right. It's amazing how the look passed from mom to her daughters. Now, as a mom, I find myself using that same facial expression with my children. And it works!

An ungrateful attitude affects not only the person expressing it, but others as well. What does it mean to have a thankful heart? Why not a thankful mouth? Or a thankful face?

What sets our mouths into motion?

Think about it. When someone is appreciative, her words uplift, encourage, and inspire others. Her words are evidence of a selfless and humble life. *With the tongue, we praise our Lord and Father, and with it we curse men, who have been made in God's likeness. Out of the same mouth come praise and cursing* (James 3:9-10). In other words, in the same breath, we can sing songs of praise to God and then scream at the driver in front of us. Confession time: "I am guilty as charged."

What sets our faces into motion?

*As water reflects a face, so a man's heart reflects the man.*
—Proverbs 27:19

I used to live behind a mask. Every morning, I painted on a smile. But underneath was a woman in the midst of darkness. I was one of those Christians who fell into thinking believers in Jesus couldn't be depressed and must exhibit joy at all times. Little did I know, my daily mask was slowly cracking. It worked well for a few years, but as time passed, my true feelings surfaced. A mask only works for a short time. It's a temporary fix. God calls us out from behind the veil to be real, authentic, and holy like Jesus.

What sets our hearts into motion?

*The Lord doesn't look at the things man looks at. Man looks at the outward appearance, but the Lord looks at the heart.*
—1 Samuel 16:7

In other words, we often look at the outside of a person while God focuses on the inside. Character develops within the heart of man. The more we love Jesus, the more we reflect Him in our conversations and our actions. As we seek His face, we become His reflection! It all begins in the heart. A grateful attitude reflects a thankful heart, which affects what we say and how we act. A transformed life is the result.

## LIFE CHALLENGE
Practicing God's Truths and biblical principles is the best way to apply them to our lives. So the next time you sit at the dinner table, don't focus on the delicious food, but on the love that went into making a meal and the one

who provided the food. Appreciate the one who spent time preparing, shopping, and creating the family dinner. Ask God to give you a thankful heart, one that serves and encourage others, lends a hand, shares words of affirmation, and one who is grateful in all circumstances. Live life sold out for Jesus with a heart that says, "Life is not about me, but all about Him." And remember, a grateful heart produces a thankful attitude, which in turn creates peaceful expressions and pleasant words.

## PRAYER JOURNAL

Read Psalm 100 with Psalm 98. Write out the verse that pierces your heart. Practice your thankfulness by writing a prayer of praise to God.

# CHAPTER 3

# RESTORE YOUR SOUL

*Love the Lord your God with all your heart and with all your soul and with all your mind and with all your strength.*

—Mark 12:30

W hat is the soul? How would you describe it? Growing up, I loved soul music. Why? I'm not sure, except I do know it touched me on the inside—

my soul. Once I accepted Jesus as my Savior, praise and worship music became my soul music.

In Luke 10:27, the Greek word for *soul* is *psyche*, which means the seat of feelings, desires, emotions, and affections.[3] Together yet separate from the body. Unlike the physical body, the soul doesn't perish at death. As believers in Jesus, we live forever in eternity with Him. Praise God for sending His son Jesus to rescue us from a life of despair and destruction.

Allow this section to enlighten your understanding of what it means to *Love the Lord with all your soul*. Before you read each entry—pray. Ask the Holy Spirit to reveal...

- The times when Jesus brings order to the chaos in your soul.
- How God refreshes and encourages your tired and weary soul.
- When God declares His glory in fearful situations.
- The times God shines His light in the middle of life's storms.
- When God rescues you from the depths of despair.

Praise Him before you move forward. Trust He has mighty things planned. Anticipate a sweet time in God's Word. Breathe as He restores your soul. Be inspired to live sold out for Jesus in every way.

# ~REST~
# THE HEAVENS
# DECLARE

*The heavens declare the glory of God; and the skies proclaim the work of His hands. Day after day they bring forth speech; and night after night they display knowledge. There is no speech or language where their voice is not heard. Their voice goes out into all the earth, and their words to the ends of the world.*

—Psalm 19:1-4

Nearing His destination, Jesus sighs in relief. Rest is near. The smell of the Sea of Galilee rejuvenates His soul. Peace and quiet call to Jesus. His weary body feels the effects of the miles traveled. Looking down at His feet, He notices His swollen ankles. Bulging blisters seem to awaken every nerve in His body. He seeks a solitary resting spot. Settling down with a rock for a pillow, He closes His eyes. The sounds of the waves gently breaking on the shore play a lullaby to His soul. He releases a silent prayer...

*Father, I need some time alone with you! Time to refresh. The throngs of people drain me... physically, mentally, and spiritually. I am so tired. My spirit needs replenishing.*

He longs for the day He and His Father reunite. With another deep sigh, He falls into a sweet sleep.

A dim light peeks over the horizon, waking Jesus from His slumber. Taking a deep breath, He stretches His aching body. A craving in His Spirit overrides the rumble in His stomach. He decides to take a walk before breakfast.

Strolling along the shore brings back memories. He recalls His conversation with Peter very close to here, and He smiles at the memory. A feeling of encouragement envelops Him. Jesus scans the beauty before Him as a crisp sea breeze lifts His cloak, a gentle reminder of the days of creation. His eyes catch a glimpse of the sun casting its image on the surface of the water. What a picturesque moment. Suddenly, He remembers His prayer from the night before. He knows His Father is reminding Him of the time they spent together creating the universe. He hears the voice of His Father...

*Good Morning, My Son. I miss You. Soon You will be with Me again, sitting at My right hand. You are doing an excellent job! Keep it up. I can't wait for Your return home. But You have work to accomplish first. Continue listening to Me every minute, and I will give You the words to speak. I love You!*

With hands raised, Jesus quotes Psalm 19:4b-6...

*In the heavens, He has set a tabernacle for the sun, which is like a bridegroom coming out of his chamber, and rejoices like a strong man to run its race. Its rising is from one end of heaven, and its circuit to the other end; And there is nothing hidden from its heat.*

A calmness spreads over the sea. A tender touch from the Father. Answered prayer. Refreshment for His soul. Encouragement to keep going. United as one.

## LIFE CHALLENGE
Does your walk with Jesus need replenishing? Are you tired, worn out, and weary? Ask God to refresh you. Recognize the times during the day when He gives you a touch of encouragement. Rest in Him. Trust His provision. Take shelter under His wings.

## PRAYER JOURNAL
Read Psalm 19. Write out the verse that speaks to you. Journal your prayer of praise.

# ~ENCOURAGEMENT~
# GOD'S GLORY

*For God, who said, "Let light shine out of darkness," made His light shine in our hearts to give us the light of the knowledge of the glory of God in the face of Christ.*

—2 Corinthians 4:6

Mission trip. Team preparation. Crowded streets. Perfect storm. All for God's glory.

Years ago our family joined a short-term mission team serving in a poor area of Santo Domingo, Dominican Republic. Many people in this impoverished community hungered for God's love, grace, and mercy. Every night our team hosted an evangelistic crusade in the streets. The local men built a temporary stage from scrap wood and old building materials. It was the perfect opportunity to practice trust and faith in God. Every evening these thoughts popped in—*Will the stage hold all the sound equipment, musical instruments, band members, and preacher? Oh, Lord, please direct your angels to bring stability to this dilapidated structure called a stage!*

The electricity connections to the stage generated another level of faith for me. Electricity sharing between buildings was the norm. A cobweb of electrical wires hung in every direction. Each evening the locals pirated the electricity from a line somewhere above the stage. With intensity I prayed for this web of wires to stay in place.

On the last day of the mission trip, the skies opened, and rain poured. Our team debated whether to cancel the scheduled crusade. After much prayer, we decided to continue. The stage was erected, the electricity was bootlegged, and the final service commenced. Watching my two high school boys playing guitars in the praise band blessed me beyond words. Joy filled the air. Until...

A clap of thunder escaped the heavens, and a bolt of lightning flashed across the sky. Like exploding fireworks, electrical sparks burst in all directions. Fear permeated my whole body. Catching a glimpse of the wobbly stage, I closed my eyes and boldly prayed, *Please, God, stop the rain! In the name above all names, Jesus, please calm the storm brewing above. These people need to hear about Jesus, and my boys need Your safe hand of protection.*

Opening my eyes, I couldn't believe the sight! The clouds parted, and the moon peeked through as if God were saying, "Trust me. See My glory. I hold heaven and earth in the palm of My hand." In that moment, I could almost hear the Halleluiah Chorus singing, "Glory to God in the highest…"

Later that evening, I discovered that I wasn't the only one praying for God to intervene and protect us. Others on our team prayed this same prayer. God used this experience to grow our faith in Him. Prayer fueled faith into action.

## LIFE CHALLENGE

Do you recognize God's glory? Do you acknowledge His glory when facing fearful, uncomfortable situations? Take the challenge and ask God to reveal His glory in and through your life circumstances—marriage, family, finances, relationships, health, inner struggles, weaknesses, temptations, etc. Then trust Him to make Himself known in real and personal ways.

Write down your experiences, so you don't forget. In all your ways, live sold out for Him.

## PRAYER JOURNAL

Read 2 Corinthians 5. Write out the verse that stands out to you. Journal your thoughts or a God's Glory experience.

# ~PEACE~
# UNEXPECTED
# STORMS

*God is our refuge and strength, an ever-present help in trouble. Therefore we will not fear, though the earth gives way and the mountains fall into the heart of the sea, though its waters roar and foam and the mountains quake with their surging.*

—Psalm 46:1-3

An unexpected storm. A sudden disturbance. Gale-force winds. Like a whirling tornado, an unforeseen life situation turns your world upside down. In a split second, your thoughts reel out of control. The result— discouragement, oppression, and despair.

Opening God's Word sets your heart at ease. Your eyes rest on Psalm 46. For a moment, peace flows. Yet in the back of your mind, the memory of this unexpected storm remains. Thoughts rush in. The need to control comes into play—your spouse, children, extended family, friends, work, finances, church decisions, the government, and world events. In your mind's eye, life appears bleak. Once again you glance down at your Bible...

*There is a river whose streams make glad the city of God, the holy place where the Most High dwells. God is within her, she will not fall; God will help her at break of day. Nations are in uproar, kingdoms fall; He lifts his voice, the earth melts. The LORD Almighty is with us; the God of Jacob is our fortress.*

—Psalm 46: 4-7

The words gently calm your spirit...

*Come and see the works of the LORD, the desolations He has brought on the earth. He makes wars cease to the ends of the earth; He breaks the bow and shatters the spear, He burns the chariots with fire.*

—Psalm 46: 8-9

Stillness falls. God's Word slowly begins changing your perspective. *Come and see the works of the Lord. He makes... He breaks... He burns...!* You believe God. You trust He is in control. He is everywhere, and no one can hide from Him. He knows everything all the time. Yes, even your unexpected storm.

Your heart fills with joy. In the midst of reading the final verses of Psalm 46, humbleness envelops your soul…

*"Be still, and know that I am God; I will be exalted among the nations, I will be exalted in the earth." The LORD Almighty is with us; the God of Jacob is our fortress.*
—Psalm 46: 10-11

Dropping to your knees, you thank God for what He is doing through this unforeseen situation. A fresh thought ignites—*just as the sun peaks through the clouds in the midst of a storm, so the Son of God shines His light in the middle of life's disturbances*. Peace flows. You trust in His provision. You believe He is in control. And, above all, you acknowledge His love for you in and through your unexpected storm.

## LIFE CHALLENGE

When experiencing unexpected storms, remember to run to Psalm 46. Surrender it all to Jesus. Trust and know that God is with you, shining His light through your stormy situations. Pray for opportunities to share Psalm 46 with others and don't forget to live sold out for Him. It's all about Him and not about us.

## PRAYER JOURNAL

Read Psalm 46. Write out the verse that captures your heart. Journal your prayer of praise.

# ~Rescue~
# Under The
# Surface

*Save me, O God, for the waters have come up to my neck. I sink in the miry depths, where there is no foothold. I have come into the deep waters; the floods engulf me. I am worn out calling for help; my throat is parched. My eyes fail, looking for my God.*

—Psalm 69:1-3

A picturesque day at the beach. A much-needed vacation. The warmth of the sun beams down. The feel of the sand soothes the soul. Breathing deep activates a calm spirit. It's the ideal setting for a perfect day.

No one suspects. No one imagines. Out in the deep, far beneath the ocean's surface, a storm brews. A rumble from the bottom of the ocean bellows its way through the silence of the waters. From the shore, no one notices until…

A scream echoes across the sand. The onlookers point toward the water. Turning, you see a very large wave on the horizon. Surfers dash to grab their boards, in hopes of catching the rides of their lives. But then, you notice a drastic change. Water is pulling away from the beach. Someone screams, "Tsunami!"

Like ants rushing to protect their bed, people scamper in all directions. Parents move in high gear. They grab their crying children and run for higher ground. Others remain motionless, paralyzed in shock. Some don't care who is in the way. A stampede erupts. The water suddenly reverses direction again with unbelievable speed and crashes onshore, consuming the beach, engulfing the land beyond, and leaving unbelievable devastation. The world feels the impact of this disaster.

How do we relate to a faraway tsunami? What spiritual truths can we glean from this real life catastrophe?

Sometimes, on the surface, everything appears in order. But, underneath, an earthquake rumbles. Perhaps a shift occurs because of a death, a divorce, the loss of a job, financial problems, depression, health issues, a rebellious child or some other troubled relationship. We try to hold our emotions inside. Suppress them. Stuff them. But like a tidal wave, these feelings eventually spill out when least expected—flooding our thoughts, crashing our expectations, and throwing our lives into chaos.

How can we recover from utter confusion or out of control circumstances? Let God help. Just like federal agencies send in relief teams to assist after a natural disaster, God sends His rescue teams into our lives when we need them. Sometimes the help comes in the form of prayer warriors, the Holy Spirit's intercession, or even a miracle. Maybe it is a change of heart, an attitude adjustment, financial help, or the right doctor. Perhaps it is as simple as an encouraging word, a hug, or a meal. Recognize Jesus in the midst of it all. Give everything over to Him. Trust Him. Praise Him. Let your soul rest in Him. He loves you.

## LIFE CHALLENGE

Is there an underground rumbling going on in your life? Does everything appear normal although turmoil is building? Read Psalm 69:14 for relief—*Rescue me from the mire, do not let me sink. Deliver me from those who hate me, from the deep waters. Do not let the floodwaters engulf me, or the depths swallow me up or the pit close its mouth over me.* Let God's Word wash over you. Trust Him. Believe His Word. Open your arms and surrender it all to Him. In the midst of the strife, live sold out for Jesus.

## PRAYER JOURNAL

Read Psalm 69. Write out the verse that impacts your heart. Journal your prayer.

# ~ORDER~
# DISCOVERING
# LIGHT

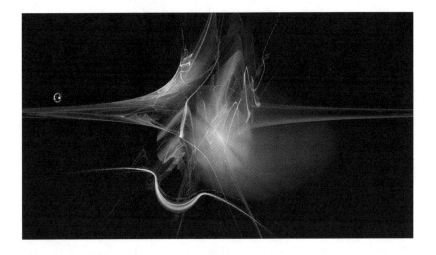

*In the beginning God created the heavens and the earth. The earth was without form, and void; and darkness was on the face of the deep. And the Spirit of God was hovering over the face of the waters. Then God said, "Let there be light," and there was light. And God saw the light that it was good; and God divided the light from the darkness.*

—Genesis 1:1-3 (NKJV)

Go beyond the obvious. Look for the hidden treasures. God's Word uses tangible objects to teach spiritual life lessons. For example, the account of God's creation is packed with spiritual analogies. Close your eyes and pray for the Lord to open your heart to fresh insights. Let the Holy Spirit bring understanding to God's Word.

*In the beginning, God created the heavens and the earth.*

God designed. God fashioned. God formed. Imagine watching God's plan unfold. From Genesis 1:26, we know Jesus and the Holy Spirit were with God at the time of creation. Do you think Jesus and the Holy Spirit encouraged God as He implemented His plan? Possibly the angels served as God's cheer team, singing praises to our Lord on High. How fun to think beyond the obvious.

*The earth was without form, and void.*

How would you describe the image at the beginning of this section, Discovering Light? Formless, chaotic, empty, disordered, disorganized, turbulent, out of control? Imagine the earth during this time.

*Darkness was on the face of the deep.*

*Darkness*—was it physical or spiritual? Maybe *the deep* was another name for the abyss, a place void of God. Perhaps *darkness* represented the evil covering the abyss. No light. Total emptiness. God's spirit was absent.

*The Spirit of God was hovering over the face of the waters.*

Imagine the Spirit of God suspended over the waters. God perceived it all. He saw through the darkness. From the outer edges of the chaos, He looked beyond the surface of the deep. God was on the verge of releasing His plan for the earth and all mankind.

Then, like a crescendo in the heavens, God speaks…

*Let there be light, and there was light and it was good.*

The Earth was without form—dark, empty, and void of beauty until God breathed light into existence. For out of the darkness, light appeared.

However, if the sun was yet to be created, what was the light?

Could it be that God's glory was the light illuminating the earth? Without a shadow of a doubt, I shout, "Yes, and glory in the highest!" The beginning of creation is symbolic of our need for a Savior. Without Jesus, the human soul exists in a state of confusion, disorder, and spiritual darkness. But the moment someone trusts in Jesus as Lord and Savior, Jesus' light wipes out the darkness. A person, who once could not understand the things of God, now shines with Christ's light forevermore.

*The city does not need the sun or the moon to shine on it, for the glory of God gives it light, and the Lamb is its lamp.*

—Revelation 21:23

## LIFE CHALLENGE

Are you in the midst of a chaotic situation? Is your life spinning out of control? God is still in the business of bringing order out of chaos. Give it all to Jesus. Ask Him to bring your turbulence into the Light, so you see things through His eyes. Ask others to pray for you. Prayer is one way God allows His children to participate in eternity here on earth. Watch what He begins to do in your life, and give Him glory before you see results.

## PRAYER JOURNAL

Read Genesis 1:1-3 with John 1:1-5. Journal your thoughts on light versus darkness. Ask God to show you a fresh perspective.

# CHAPTER 4
# RENEW YOUR MIND

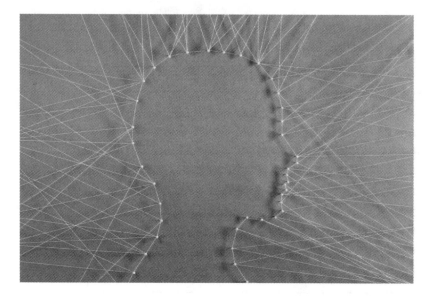

*Love the Lord your God with all your heart and with all your soul and with all your **mind** and all your strength.*

— Mark 12:30

Love the Lord with all your *mind*? What does your *mind* have to do with your spiritual life? How is it possible to love God with your *mind*? The Greek word for *mind*, in Mark 12:30, is *dianoia,* which means the place in the brain that understands, feels, and thinks. This area of the brain discerns, perceives, and distinguishes thoughts—good or bad.[4] Now we are getting somewhere.

How many thoughts do you have in a day?

A thousand?
One hundred thousand?
A zillion?

Thoughts constantly bombard our minds—positive and negative. Filling our minds with God's Word, praise and worship music, conversations with God, and godly discussions with others helps us to stay focused on Jesus. Asking God to help change your thought life to a prayer life is crucial for your spiritual wellbeing.

Take a deep breath, close your eyes, and pray. Ask the Holy Spirit to clear your mind of any worries, fears, burdens, or even daily agendas. Focus on His Word. Open your heart and mind to all He has for you. Look for these truths sprinkled throughout this chapter...

- Abide – As we remain in Him, we can give true love to others.
- Repent – Accept His gift of forgiveness.
- Release – Let God shine into the dark places.
- Trust – Follow, listen, believe.
- Laughter – Let God teach spiritual lessons through humorous times.

Enjoy renewing your mind as you live sold out for Jesus.

# ~ABIDE~
# LOVE DEEP

*As the Father loved Me, I also have loved you; abide in My love. If you keep My commandments, you will abide in My love, just as I have kept My Father's commandments and abide in His love. These things I have spoken to you, that My joy may remain in you, and that your joy may be full. This is My commandment, that you love one another as I have loved you.*

*Greater love has no one than this, to lay down one's life for his friends.*

—John 15:9-13 (NKJV)

L ove is in the air.

How do you define *love?* Do you *feel love* or are you *in love?* What's the difference? Think for a few moments. Where did you learn the meaning of love—from your parents, grandparents, spouse, church, friends, television, the movies, magazines, books, or even from commercials?

As defined by the world, love seems to focus on the receiver. However, the Word of God projects an entirely different meaning. Studying the Bible's original text and examining the root words opens the door to deeper meanings. Notice in John 15: 9-13 (NKJV), the word *love* is used eight times. The Greek word here is *agape,* which gives the idea of brotherly love, affection, good will, or benevolence.[5] The focus is on the heart of the giver rather than the receiver. God desires for His children to unconditionally love each other. Not out of duty. Not from a command. But from a heart that says, "You don't owe me a thing."

Now, we are getting somewhere. Also embedded within John 15:9-13 is the word *abide.* In order to understand the fullness of these verses, it is vital to grasp the meaning of this word. In the Greek, *abide* means to remain as one, not to become another or different.[6] Jesus isn't calling us to follow rules and regulations, but to remain as one in His love. He doesn't chain us to Himself.

He offers us choices. As we love Jesus with our hearts, souls, minds, and strength, our relationships with Him deepen. Our lives are affected. As a result, our thought processes conform to His. We are changed from the inside out. This love creates a ripple effect...

God dearly loves Jesus... Jesus dearly loves me... So I dearly love others.

Jesus' words, *Greater love has no one than this, to lay down one's life for his friends,* bring me to my knees. Jesus viewed His death on the cross as an act of love for His friends — past, present, and future. That includes you and me! Wow, true love is unconditional, selfless, sacrificial, and pure.

## LIFE CHALLENGE

Choose to experience the warmth of God's love by abiding in Jesus. Allow Him to renew your mind through prayer, reading His Word, and applying His truths. Share what God is doing in and through your life with others through a smile, a prayer, an act of giving, forgiving others, or in whatever way the Lord directs. Then, expect to experience John 15:11... *These things I have spoken to you, that My joy may remain in you, and that your joy may be full.* There is nothing like the joy of the Lord as you live sold out for Him.

## PRAYER JOURNAL

Read John 15:1-17. Write out the verse that touches your heart. Memorize it. Journal your prayer of love to the Father.

# ~Surrender~
# Inside The Walls
# Of Guilt

*Restore to me the joy of your salvation and grant me a willing spirit, to sustain me.*

—Psalm 51:12

The following is a short story God poured into my heart after praying for a friend held captive by guilt, shame, and blame.

*** 

## Inside the Walls of Guilt

Desire for Grace. Freedom in Forgiveness.

Disgrace permeates my mind. Humiliation runs through my veins. My shameful actions seem too great for God to forgive. Once again, I cry out in distress, "God help me let go and fully trust you!" Reluctantly, I grasp my Bible and turn to Psalm 51:1-5…

*Have mercy upon me, O God, according to Your unfailing love; according to Your great compassion blot out my transgressions. Wash away all my iniquity and cleanse me from my sin. For I know my transgressions, and my sin is always before me. Against You, You only, have I sinned and done what is evil in your sight.*

These dingy, gray walls of guilt hold me captive to my past. Gazing outside the window, I long for the freshness of spring, the warmth of the sun, and the freedom to run through the meadow. How do I break free from my soiled past? My eyes fix on the next few verses…

*Surely you desire truth in the inner parts; you teach me wisdom in the inmost place. Cleanse me with hyssop, and I will be clean; wash me, and I will be whiter than snow. Let me hear joy and gladness; let the bones you have crushed rejoice. Hide your face*

*from my sins and blot out all my iniquity. Create in me a pure heart, O God, and renew a steadfast spirit within me. Do not cast me from your presence or take your Holy Spirit from me.*
— Psalm 51: 6-11

Weeping, sobbing, kneeling before the Lord, I ask, "Are You sure You can create a pure heart in me? I desire this so much. For years, these grimy, stained walls encircled my mind. This darkness closes in more and more each day. Time is fleeting. I want out, but can't find the exit. I don't deserve freedom from this hopeless dungeon of guilt. My sin is too great to merit Your forgiveness. But… I **trust** Your Word. I **trust** in Your forgiveness.

With tears streaming, I open my arms, take in a deep breath, and say, "Surrender—I surrender all." Suddenly my soul is renewed. Something releases. The chains unlock, and I feel a sense of freedom. I read the rest of Psalm 51: 12-19 out loud…

*Restore to me the joy of your salvation and grant me a willing spirit, to sustain me. Then I will teach transgressors your ways, and sinners will turn back to you. Save me from bloodguilt, O God, the God who saves me, and my tongue will sing of your righteousness. O Lord, open my lips, and my mouth will declare your praise. You do not delight in sacrifice, or I would bring it; you do not take pleasure in burnt offerings. The sacrifices of God are a broken spirit; a broken and contrite heart, Oh God, you will not despise. In your good pleasure make Zion prosper; build up the walls of Jerusalem. Then there will be righteous sacrifices, whole burnt offerings to delight you; the bulls will be offered on your altar.*

Scanning the room, I notice a wide open door—a door I never noticed before. I hear the Lord say, "My child, this door of forgiveness is always present. But your years of guilt built layers and layers of debris, covering this passageway to freedom. I've been waiting to free you, but you needed to see yourself as I see you. Forgiven—past, present, and future. I love you and long to experience an intimate relationship with you."

Immediately, the sweet aroma of springtime travels through the doorway. I breathe in this fragrance of forgiveness—God's forgiveness! Tears pour. Heart warms. Humbleness flows. The once bleak and dreary walls now appear white as snow. Praises erupt. I thank Jesus for His grace and mercy. Examining this restoration process leaves me humbled and amazed.

*Inside the walls of guilt is a desire for grace and freedom in forgiveness.*

\*\*\*

As a Christian speaker, I hear this story over and over. Many people have a difficult time accepting God's complete forgiveness. They live bonded to their tarnished pasts and unwise choices. This acceptance becomes Satan's battlefield where he ambushes the mind with fiery darts of guilt, lies, and accusations. Surrendering it all to Jesus frees us from our past.

## LIFE CHALLENGE

Can you relate? Maybe you know someone who struggles with forgiving herself of past or present sins such as addiction, verbal abuse, abortion, sexual sin, an affair, gossip, rebellion, eating disorder, self-absorption, materialism, judgment of others, legalism, or something else. We like to categorize our sins. We think God views some sins greater than others. The fact is "sin is sin" to God. He is waiting for us not only to repent of our sins, but also to surrender our guilt and accept His gift of forgiveness. Experience His forgiveness today. Like Psalm 51:17 says, *The sacrifices of God are a broken spirit; a broken and contrite heart.*

## PRAYER JOURNAL

Read Psalm 51. Write out the verse that touches your heart. Confess your sins before the Lord. Walk forward knowing you are freed from the past. Journal your prayer.

# ~RELEASE~
# SPIRITUAL JUNK
# CLOSETS

*How much more, then, will the blood of Christ, who through the eternal Spirit offered himself unblemished to God, cleanse our consciences from acts that lead to death, so that we may serve the living God!*

—Hebrews 9:14

J unk closets—those special hideaway niches for all the unwanted clutter. Maybe this is the place you store those old, worn-out items and things you don't know what to do with. Over time, the buildup can be overwhelming.

In my Bible study, *Reflecting Him*, I invite readers to take a guided tour through various rooms in their homes and compare these areas to their spiritual lives. The first day of the tour focuses on the junk closet—that hidden, dark place no one enters but you. "Out of sight, out of mind" might describe those items tucked away in this darkened space.

"Out of sight, out of mind" could also refer to parts of our spiritual lives, the things we hide in our minds and hearts: past hurts, painful experiences, guilt, selfish acts, unwise choices, and even negative thoughts. When we clean out our junk closets, we bring order back into our homes. Putting our spiritual lives in order gives us a fresh start too. The result—God replaces the clutter and debris with His love, grace, forgiveness, and mercy.

In many cases, a professional closet organizer might give you some new ideas to help in the reorganization of the storage area in your home, such as special shelving or extra containers. Likewise, we need help cleaning out our spiritual closets. For believers, the Bible offers us an organizational plan and the Holy Spirit helps us implement it.

## LIFE CHALLENGE

Do you harbor bitterness from past hurts? Does sin linger in the closets of your heart and mind? Are you in need of

God's forgiveness? Let go and let God shine His light into these darkened areas. Let Him release you from the pain, anguish, and suffering of silence. Take a few minutes and ask God to reveal any spiritual junk closets in your life. Listen to His voice. Heed His answer. Release your pride. Allow Him access to every area of your life. With anticipation, sit back and enjoy the experience of a fresh, clean, spiritual closet.

## PRAYER JOURNAL

Read Hebrews 9:14 with 1 John 1:5-10. Light penetrates the darkness. Jesus is the Light. Write out the verse that touches your heart. Journal your prayer of praise.

# ~BELIEVE~
# GOD'S VOICE

*Let the morning bring me word of Your unfailing love, for I have put my trust in You. Show me the way I should go, for to You I lift up my soul.*

—Psalm 143:8

I was anxious and excited at the same time. First of all, this was our trip of a lifetime—an Alaskan cruise. Also, this was the starting point of my first writing project—*Reflecting Him: The Touch of the Potter*. The first morning of the cruise, I found a quiet location, opened my laptop, and started writing. What a breathtaking place to write about God as the Creator of all things. I found myself captivated by the snowcapped mountains, spellbound by a whale breaking the surface of the water, and awestruck by a bald eagle gracefully soaring overhead. A sense of peace permeated my soul.

Without thinking, I started praising God out loud. The blessings of my surroundings, mixed with researching the pottery process and comparing the potter to God as the Creator, put a song of praise in my heart. Silent prayer erupted...

*God, are You sure You want me to write this Bible study? You know I don't consider myself a writer. In fact, I don't know what I'm doing. However, I hear Your voice calling me to write. I trust in You. I believe You can do, through me, what I can't do myself. But, please give me some kind of confirmation. Amen.*

As the morning waned, I noticed a crowd of people collecting in one area of the deck. I closed my laptop and maneuvered my way through the throng of onlookers. At last, I stood before an unbelievable sight. A man, sitting at a potter's wheel, was forming a vessel from a wet lump of clay. My mouth dropped. I couldn't believe it! As I collected my thoughts, I heard him say, "The lump of clay cannot change form until the potter's hands gently take hold of it." Even now tears emerge. Humbleness flows.

God answered my prayer in His perfect timing. In His infinite way of working things for His glory, He orchestrated a divine appointment for me on a cruise ship off the coast of Alaska. During my moment of doubt, He confirmed His call upon my life. This experience became a stepping stone for my writing process. I am so thankful we serve an almighty God who wants to be part of our everyday lives.

## LIFE CHALLENGE

Listen. Trust. Believe. Do you find it difficult to discern God's voice? Do you trust Him in all areas of your life? Do you believe God's Word even when it doesn't make sense? Keeping your eyes on Christ takes the focus off of you and puts it onto Him. God has a plan for you to help accomplish His Kingdom purposes. Follow Him closely. Listen. Trust His voice. Believe He will provide. Look for Him in the midst of your day. Keep your eyes open to the tender moments the Lord has in store. Choose to live every moment sold out for Jesus.

## PRAYER JOURNAL

Read Romans 12, focusing on verse 2, and Psalm 143:8. Write out the verse God places on your heart. Journal your prayers and thoughts.

# ~LAUGH~
# GOD'S MEDICINE

*A cheerful heart is good medicine, but a crushed spirit dries up the bones.*

—Proverbs 17:22

Laughter is the body's best medicine. Laughter is the shortest distance between two people. Laughter is an instant vacation.

Through the years, I recall hearing these statements. I'm not sure how true they are, but each definition leads me to believe a sense of humor brings positive results. Learning to laugh is a skill—or is it?

Some people might think of laughter as an action or sound. Others might describe laughter as a vocal burst of air with interesting facial and body movements. Another might define the word laughter as an eruption of noises from the vocal cords causing others to join in. No matter the explanation, one thing is certain—laughter is almost always contagious.

For some odd reason, things happen to me that make other people laugh, a lot! A close, lifelong friend once said, "Carla, I think the Lord allows all these funny moments in your life so you can use them as spiritual teaching lessons for your speaking engagements." Well, if you have heard me speak at an event, you know I have plenty of teaching lessons to use. Let me illustrate my point.

With my head still on my pillow, I thanked God for the day ahead. Excitement filled my heart. It was my first day to teach my *Reflecting Him Bible Study* to approximately 150 women at a large church in The Woodlands, Texas. I started praying over the women, asking God to connect our hearts. I meditated on the focus verse (2 Corinthians 3:18) for *Reflecting Him*...

*And we, who with unveiled faces all reflect the Lord's glory, are being transformed into His likeness with ever-increasing glory, which comes from the Lord, who is the Spirit.*

I climbed out from under the covers and stumbled into the bathroom. With my vision still blurry, I glanced into the mirror. Something caught my attention. Leaning in for a better look, my mouth dropped open, and I screamed, "My face is falling off!" Bewildered. Confused. Dismayed. I suddenly remembered that two days before, a dear friend performed a chemical peel on my face. Her new job required her to use the peel treatment on a few clients before she received her certification. Since this procedure was at no cost to me, I eagerly volunteered. Little did I know, she loved me enough to add a booster to the process. All I can say is, "It worked!" For a brief second, my mind spun out of control. *The women probably won't even notice. I could call in sick and not show up. I could walk in at the last minute and leave after the Amen.*

But reality set in as God reminded me of the purpose of *Reflecting Him*—to recognize the spiritual life lessons He gives us every day. God continually reminds me of how important it is to be real and authentic at all of my speaking engagements. Needless to say, I was a living example of the focus verse... *with unveiled faces.* I am not kidding. My face continued to peel all morning long. I couldn't just ignore it, and my story caused the whole class to experience the true meaning of laughter. The room was filled with giggles, chuckles, and realness!

Yes, God answered my prayer and connected our hearts. I smile as I think about the creative ways God works things to His glory.

## LIFE CHALLENGE

Ask the Lord to bring some laughter into your life. Of course, I am not talking about laughing **at** people. I am encouraging genuine, pure humor that causes you to experience the joy of the Lord. I know God has a sense of humor. Think about it—in Numbers 22:28, God allowed a donkey to talk! Look for opportunities to laugh and smile. Let Him teach you spiritual lessons through the humorous moments in life as you live sold out for Him.

## PRAYER JOURNAL

Read Psalm 33 with Proverbs 17:22. Write out your favorite verse from this chapter. Journal your prayers and thoughts.

# CHAPTER 5
# REBUILD YOUR
# STRENGTH

*Love the Lord your God with all your heart and with all your soul and with all your mind and all your strength.*

—Mark 12:30

L ove the Lord with all your strength? How can our muscles love the Lord? Seriously, that doesn't make sense. Or does it? The Greek word for strength in Mark 12:30 is *ischys*, which means the ability, force, might.[7] By loving the Lord with all our strength, we love Him with our abilities, skills, and talents. For example, when teaching a Sunday school or Bible study class, instead of just focusing on the lesson, subject matter, and delivery, we need to set our eyes on Jesus. Rather than saying begrudgingly, "It's my turn to teach the lesson this week," ask God to help you change your attitude so your focus is on Him, not the task at hand. Jesus enables us to use our abilities and talents to glorify God.

When we call upon Jesus to do in us what only He can do, He gets the glory. As you read this chapter, focus on serving the Lord with all your strength, through His power and might, as you live for Him. Be inspired to…

- Read God's Word and pray daily.
- Ask God to be in the middle of your relationships.
- Ask God to set your daily agenda.
- Ask God to help you think before you speak.
- Pray for God to draw your children to an intimate relationship with Him.

Please pray before you read each section. Ask the Lord to inspire your journey as you renew your strength and live sold out for Him.

# ~SPIRITUAL LIFE~
# BALANCING ACT

*Who has measured the waters in the hollow of His hand, or with the breadth of His hand marked off the heavens? Who has held the dust of the earth in a basket, or weighed the mountains on the scales and the hills in a balance?*

—Isaiah 40:12

No way! I don't believe what I'm seeing.

How does she balance the basket on her head and then walk as if she is in a race?

While strolling the streets of Antigua, Guatemala, these thoughts constantly ran through my mind. Everywhere I turned, another *balancing act* was on display.

After returning home from my mission trip, these images popped into my head for days. So, in the privacy of my home, I decided to try it myself. I retrieved a decorative basket from the top of my kitchen cabinet. It seemed just the right size for my head. Feeling confident, I gracefully put the basket on top of my head and released my hands. It wobbled a bit, but then steadied. With growing confidence, I stepped forward. The basket toppled to the ground. Laughing at myself, I kept trying, and suddenly the idea hit me that the basket needed some weight to press it into my head. Feeling hopeful, I filled it with towels, put the basket on my head again, stretched out my arms for balance, and took a step. The basket slipped off again. I'm still in awe of the women in Antigua who perform this task so effortlessly.

As I worked through these thoughts and frustrations, God opened my eyes to a spiritual lesson: these women practice balancing a basket on their heads from an early age. They know which basket works best for the different things they carry, and they understand the importance of shifting the contents around to achieve the perfect balance. They also know how to cushion the baskets to allow for bumps along the way.

This analogy is like the Christian life. In order to maintain balance in our spiritual lives, we need to practice spending time in the Word. God knows which baskets we need each day. When we spend time with Him at the beginning of the day, He spiritually fills us, giving us the padding and protection we need.

Sometimes our spiritual baskets are initially weighted appropriately, but throughout the day, we add things like worry, fear, frustration, or anger. These emotions produce a shift in the weight and add pressure, creating an unbalanced load. Prayer attacks this problem. Giving it all to Jesus rebalances our loads, allowing us to accomplish His plans and purposes.

## LIFE CHALLENGE

Each morning, allow God to fill your spiritual basket. He knows what your day holds. Be aware of the extra things you might add to it. Walk on, knowing He is protecting you from bumps along the way. Practice this daily and enjoy the balancing act.

## PRAYER JOURNAL

Read Isaiah 40. Write out the verse or verses that spur your spirit. Write out ways to live sold out for Jesus by applying these verses to your life.

Sold Out: Live for Jesus

# ~Numbers~
# A Cord Of Three

*Two are better than one, because they have a good return for their work: If one falls down, his friend can help him up... Though one may be overpowered, two can defend themselves. A cord of three strands is not quickly broken.*

—Ecclesiastes 4:9, 10, 12

Over thirty years of marriage? No way! Where did the years go? Looking back, God's presence in our marriage is very evident.

Our love story began in high school. By the hand of God, I moved to Abilene, Texas, my senior year and attended Wylie High School. Fred and I met in a class called Home and Family Living. I should have realized Fred's family man potential from the start. Why? Because, at the end of the year, he was awarded Who's Who in Home and Family Living. He finally asked me on a date halfway through the year. Of course, I said, "Yes." Throughout the evening, this thought played over and over in my head, *There's something different about this guy.* Not only was he cute, in modern terms *hot*, his sense of humor also captivated my heart. Almost immediately, a spark burst into a flame.

Time moved on, and I followed Fred to Aggieland — Texas A&M University. We married the summer before our senior year. We saved just enough money to make it through the year, or so we thought. In fact, our humorous stories of "making it" are foundational for strengthening our marriage.

Through our dating years, our wedding, college graduations, career choices, and raising our four children, life seemed to move so fast. Now over thirty years later, Jesus continues to be our solid rock. He provides strength through the wonderful times and the tough times. Honestly, when I think of our marriage, a cord of three strands comes to mind — Fred, me, and the third strand, which consists of the Father, the Son, and the Holy Spirit, all in one.

Be encouraged. Intertwine your marriage with the third

strand. This cord provides the strength your marriage needs when the world, the enemy, and the things of the flesh are working to pull it apart. It is exciting to know God is the one holding the marriage together.

## LIFE CHALLENGE

Try this experiment. Take one strand of thread and hold it with both hands. Pull as hard as you can. What happens? It quickly breaks. Now, twist two strands of thread together and pull. What happens? Again, it's easily broken. For the ultimate challenge, twist three strands of thread together and give a big pull. What happens? Why does that third strand make a difference?

Ask God to be the third strand in all of your relationships. Praise Him for providing strength, direction, and power in your life. Live sold out for Him as you work together and stand in the gap for others.

## PRAYER JOURNAL

Read Ecclesiastes 4:9-12. Write out these verses. Journal a prayer of praise for our Lord, the third strand.

# ~BUSYNESS~
# THE SUPER-HERO
# SYNDROME

*In all your ways acknowledge Him, and He will make your paths straight.*

—Proverbs 3:6

I can handle it. I've done it before, and I can do it again. No, thank you, I have it under control.

Have these thoughts ever crossed your mind? Better yet, can you remember them rolling off your tongue? We live in the era of superheroes like Wonder Woman and Batman. In fact, when our children were younger, they called me Mighty Mom. Too many times, women think they can handle it all—husbands, children, jobs, Bible studies, shopping, laundry, cooking, carpooling, children's activities, community events, and more.

I remember a time when I dressed myself in the wardrobe of Wonder Woman—Mighty Mom. Not only did I think I could do it all, I believed the lie. I was *supposed* to do it all!

Let me set the scene…

After ten years of marriage, I had learned to play the superhero role with excellence. Along with home-schooling our four young children, I was teaching a Bible study and serving as the AWANA commander at our church. My daily routine consisted of teaching, cooking, cleaning, laundry, carpooling, disciplining, and the list went on and on.

Yes, I played the role of a superhero well, or so people thought. Every time I walked out of my house, I put on the Wonder Woman—Mighty Mom mask. I wore it with pride. I was a woman who could get things done. In my mind, I was doing everything for the Lord. But in reality, my daily accomplishments became my idol. What I achieved through the day developed into my quest and pursuit.

Little did I know, I was on a slippery slope leading to

the darkest time in my life, the pit of depression. On the outside everything appeared in order—spiritual life, marriage, children, friends, health. Yet inside, the feeling of death simmered… not a physical death, but a living death. My joy slowly faded into the darkness. Thoughts emerged like, *But I'm a Christian. I love Jesus. What is wrong with me? Why do I feel this way? How can I have these thoughts?* No one knew, not even my husband. In fact, my marriage teetered back and forth. Laughter withered away. To my way of thinking, our problems existed because of him.

On top of it all, mothering four young children required love, discipline, and steadfastness. I knew they needed me. But, the superhero costume wasn't working any longer. One night, after tucking my children into bed, I turned off the lights and curled up in the corner of the playroom. I cried out over and over, *God help!* Tears poured. This is all I prayed and all God wanted—my surrendered heart.

I praise the Lord, because in His perfect timing, He pulled me from the darkness of despair. With the help of my doctor, my husband, and prayer warriors, God healed me. I now share my story for His glory.

Please learn from my experience. In my twenties and thirties, I suffered from the super-hero syndrome. I lived with an "all about me and what I could accomplish" attitude. In fact, I thought God needed me to do all these things for Him. But, He didn't need me. He longed for me to surrender it all to Him and live sold out for Jesus. Once I submitted to Him and gave up the superhero costume,

God was able to work in and through my life to affect His Kingdom.

## LIFE CHALLENGE

Are you trying to do it all? Before you walk out of your house, do you put on the Wonder Woman—Mighty Mom outfit? Can you feel the mask becoming a permanent part of your daily attire? The Lord doesn't call us to do it all, but to live for Him through His strength. Let Him set your daily agenda. Meditate on our focus verse, Proverbs 3:6... *In all your ways acknowledge Him, and He will make your paths straight.* What is God saying to you? Listen intently. Call upon His name. Wait in expectation. Live sold out for Jesus.

## PRAYER JOURNAL

Read Proverbs 3. Write out the verse that stands out to you. Journal your thoughts.

# ~CONVERSATIONS~
# FIGHTING FIRES

*Likewise the tongue is a small part of the body, but it makes great boasts. Consider what a great forest is set on fire by a small spark. The tongue also is a fire, a world of evil among the parts of the body. It corrupts the whole person, sets the whole course of his life on fire, and is itself set on fire by hell.*

—James 3:5-6

A fifty-year drought, scorching heat, gusting winds, and parched trees created the perfect recipe for disaster. It started like any other Labor Day—no school, sleeping late, and a big family breakfast.

Little did we know, lurking in a wooded area of our community, a tiny ember sparked. Within seconds, it ignited into a sea of flames. Firefighters arrived on the scene. Many neighborhoods had to be evacuated. Blockades diverted traffic to safer routes. People from all over provided evacuees and firefighters with food, supplies, water, and other necessities. What took years and years to produce was consumed within minutes.

Questions materialized. Why would God allow this tragedy? What are we to learn from this event? I turned to the Bible, and God opened my eyes to a new and fresh understanding.

Just as a small spark can set an entire forest on fire, the tongue can ignite a conversation into a blaze of hurt. One word can diffuse the situation or create a firestorm that may not be extinguishable.

*Likewise the tongue is a small part of the body, but it makes great boasts. Consider what a great forest is set on fire by a small spark. The tongue also is a fire, a world of evil among the parts of the body. It corrupts the whole person, sets the whole course of his life on fire, and is itself set on fire by hell.*

—James 3:5-6

When God teaches me something through His Word, He usually gives me an opportunity to put the lesson into practice. Sure enough, a couple of days later, God did provide an opportunity.

After completely unloading my grocery cart of thirty to forty items, I realized I was in one of those 15 items or less checkout lanes. The cashier just looked at me, and then pointed to the sign. I offered to put the groceries back in the basket and go to another aisle, but he just rolled his eyes and said, "Come on through." By this time, a woman filed in behind me. She mumbled, "I can't believe this! Don't you know you have too many items? Who do you think you are?" Embarrassed, I quickly said to her, "I am so sorry. I didn't realize this was a quick checkout lane until after I unloaded my basket." She continued to bad-mouth me. I continued apologizing. But, she didn't seem to hear me. My flesh stirred, but the Holy Spirit held back the words trying to escape my mouth. All of a sudden, I thought... *Respond with kindness.* So I looked into her eyes and said, "Thank you so much for extending grace to me even though I don't deserve it." A look of amazement appeared on her face. What could have sparked an ember into a flame was smothered by my calm response.

## LIFE CHALLENGE

Do you find yourself fighting fires or practicing fire prevention? God gives us opportunities to put His biblical principles into action. Ask the Lord to help you think before you speak. Filter all your words through Jesus. Be aware of the areas you need to surrender to the Lord. Live sold out for Jesus in and through your conversations. Remember, one word can either ignite or extinguish a spark.

## PRAYER JOURNAL

Read James 3:1-12. Write out the verse that touches your heart. Are you a *fire starter* or a *fire preventer*? Journal your prayer.

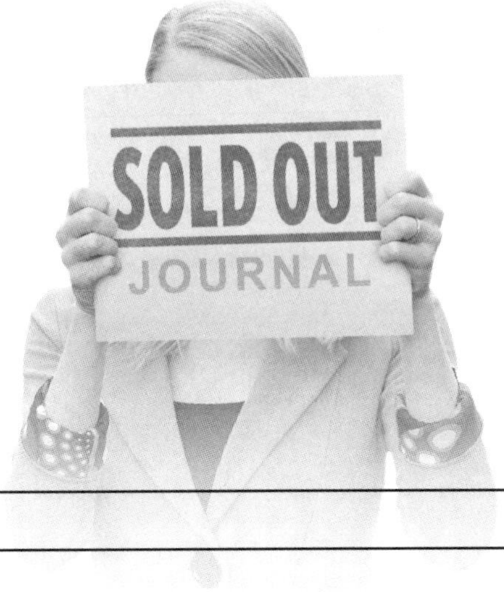
SOLD OUT
JOURNAL

# ~FAMILIES~
# TO MOM WITH
# LOVE

Carly Jo, Memom, and Carla

*Does not wisdom cry out? Does not understanding raise her voice? On the heights along the way, where the paths meet, she takes her stand; beside the gates leading into the city, at the entrances, she cries aloud: "To you, O men I call out; I raise my voice to all mankind. You who are simple, gain prudence; you who are foolish, gain understanding. Listen, for I have worthy things to say; I open my lips to speak what is right. My mouth speaks what is true, for my lips detest wickedness."*

—Proverbs 8:1-7

As moms, we long to connect with our children. A hug. A smile. A laugh. It's funny how moms continually push the memory recall button—*I remember your first step. Remember the vacation when you... It seems like yesterday when...* Do you know what I mean? In my opinion, if doctors could x-ray a mother's soul, they would find it full of sweet memories and unconditional love for her children.

When God opens a window to our children's souls, we experience inexpressible joy. Just a glimpse beyond the physical, a quick view of their spiritual growth, spurs us forward. I must share the following story with you…

When Carly Jo, the youngest of our four children, was a senior in high school, she read her English essay to me. The love and wisdom poured out on an 8.5x11 sheet of paper overwhelmed me. May the Lord bless you through Carly Jo's heart of love...

"Love, it's more than just a word or statement. Love comforts the lonely. Love feeds the hungry. Love saves a life. A child without love is like a heart without blood. How can children know how to love, if they've never been shown love themselves? Parents are the vessels used to show real love to their children.

Typically, a child's first words are "mama" or "dada."

Oh, what pride parents experience when they hear these words. Parents make the difference in a child's life. Involved parents are dedicated to teaching their children wisdom as they grow in life. They are there for them when they scrape their knees, for soccer games, piano recitals, and theater performances. They help their child realize she is a priority and special. Parents teach their children how to make wise choices early in life.

A parent's love helps nurture the child's life. But, ultimate love comes from the Father above when He gave His son Jesus to die for us and redeem us. He has such unconditional love; our human minds can't fathom how deep and how wide His love is for us. He will never leave nor forsake you. You may leave Him, but He will always be waiting for you with open arms. Allow God's love to shine through you as parents. The ultimate gift is God's love."

By Carly Jo McDougal

Tenderness enveloped my heart and soul. This essay reminded me of God's love for His children. Our Father God expresses His love to us through His Word, almost as if He writes love letters on the tablets of our hearts. The Bible is filled with encouragement, affirmation, and confirmation of His love for us. In fact, the book of John opens the door to understanding God's ultimate love gift—Jesus.

Again, praises flow. In her teenage heart, Carly Jo recognized God as the ultimate giver of true love. His truths abound throughout her essay.

Fast-forward a few years. Fred and I have moved into what the world calls, The Empty Nest. But, I choose to call it, The Place of Rest. Even now, questions arise... *Did we equip her for the real world? Will she keep Jesus the center of her life, even in college?* Again, God hears my cry, *Lord, help all my children to enter the real world armed with Jesus' love, wisdom, and truth. To love Him with all their hearts, souls, minds, and strength.*

God gives us, as parents and grandparents, the privilege to pray for our children and grandchildren. Our priority should be to pray for them to have a real, personal relationship with Jesus. To help them grasp the role of God the Father, Jesus the Son, and the Holy Spirit. The Trinity. All in one, yet individual. All the same, yet with different roles. Pray for our families to desire to live sold out for Him. In return, through prayer, our labors of love strengthen our own faith and trust in Jesus.

## LIFE CHALLENGE

Do you long to see inside your children's hearts? Ask God to open a window to their souls. Watch for ways He offers you behind-the-scene views into their lives. Be their prayer warrior throughout the day. As you clean up their messes, wash their clothes, or sit in carpool lines—pray for their relationships with Jesus. This labor of love strengthens your own walk with the Lord. And don't forget to praise God, not your children, for their spiritual growth. Let them always hear and observe you giving God the glory for all He is doing in and through their lives.

## PRAYER JOURNAL

Read Proverbs 8:1-7. Write out the verse that touches your heart. Memorize it. Journal your thoughts.

# CHAPTER 6

# REALIGN YOUR ATTITUDE

*Whatever is true, whatever is noble, whatever is right, whatever is pure, whatever is lovely, whatever is admirable, if anything is excellent or praiseworthy, think about such things. Whatever you have learned or received or heard from me, or seen in me—put it into practice. And the God of peace will be with you.*

—Philippians 4:8, 9

Why do our attitudes change from day to day? Some mornings we wake up refreshed and excited to make a full breakfast for the family. Yet, the very next day we drag ourselves out of bed grumbling and complaining.

What creates a change in our attitudes? Do our feelings dictate our viewpoints, perspectives, and ways of thinking? In other words, when we try to satisfy the flesh, do we experience rollercoaster rides—some days up and other days down?

Reading Philippians 4:8 encourages us to realign our attitudes to God's Word. We should focus on Him in everything we do and put His biblical principles into practice. This gives the Holy Spirit access to our hearts, minds, and actions. It also breeds a Christ-centered attitude instead of a self-centered focus. *Realign the Attitude* inspires the reader to…

- Move forward focusing on God.
- Listen to God in the silence.
- Follow God's directions in everything.
- Pray and trust God.
- View roadblocks as God's plan for your life.

Be inspired. Be encouraged. Be ready. May these next five entries motivate you to realign your attitude as you live sold out for Him.

# ~TRANSITIONS~
# JOURNEY TO
# CHANGES

*I have no greater joy than to hear that my children are walking in the Truth.*

—3 John 4

Adjustments. Transitions. Changes. For many, shifting from one season to another is difficult. The changeover comes in a variety of ways, such as marriage, a pregnancy, a new job, health issues, the death of a loved one, a divorce, or moving to a new town.

As for me, one of the most difficult changes was when the last of our four children left for college. Not only was Carly Jo the last to leave our home, she is also our only daughter. I dreaded the day when we would move her into her dorm at Texas A&M University. I tried to hide the inevitable and block it from my mind. However, God knew my heart.

One morning, while scanning the Internet, this image, Changes—Next Exit, popped up on my computer screen. Immediately, God stirred something deep within me. These thoughts lit up like a neon sign in my mind. *Parenting is like taking a road trip. Travelers must be aware of the road conditions and the signs. Following the map is crucial to reaching the planned destination.* I quickly opened up a blank word document and began writing…

\*\*\*

## JOURNEY TO CHANGES

Overcome with emotion. Not prepared for the inevitable. Hasn't this parenting trip just started? I'm not ready to journey to Changes! Beyond the exit I see a roadblock on the highway: Entering the Danger Zone. I have no choice but to exit NOW!

Thoughts rush in… *But I'm not prepared to travel through Changes. I thought this road was miles ahead? At least it appeared that way.*

Suddenly, I hear God's familiar, gentle voice saying...

"My daughter, My child, Changes is your only choice. If you continue on this parenting road trip at the same speed, you'll eventually crash into My roadblock. I put it there for a reason. I've allowed your children, actually My children, to ride with you on Life's Highway for the first part of their lives. Now, each one drives with Me— alone. I need you to exit. This journey to Changes will be difficult and full of twists and turns. Starting out, the scenery is barren. Yes, like a desert. Please trust me to lead you through this next phase of the parenting trip. I promise... an oasis awaits you. Follow Me closely. Thank you for guiding and directing your children to Me. Now, get ready for a new and fresh adventure.

By the way, this parenting trip is not for you to control, but Me. I've allowed you to be a big part of your children's journey. But your role is changing. I still need you to be in your children's lives, praying for them to love Me and praying for My purposes to be accomplished through them. Thank you for deciding to travel through Changes with Me. I am proud of you. Wait until you see what's on the other side of this adventure."

Without thinking, I exit the ramp to Changes. Leaving this part of the parenting trip leads to tears, heartache, and anguish. This road is all I've known. My heart's cry is to follow God's road map. I don't want to divert from His way, but my emotions fly in all directions. With hands on the wheel and my heart lifted in praise, I cry out to God...

"I never expected this journey to Changes to be so difficult. Jesus, I need you more and more each day. Help me follow You with my everything. You are the author and finisher of our family. You love my children more than I do. I trust You completely. I know we've completed this part of the parenting trip, and You have a fresh adventure ahead. Help me not live in the past, but focus on Your road map of directions—Your Word. Thank you for allowing me to mother these four children and for the blessings of being their prayer warrior. Also, help me not miss the scenery on this journey to Changes. I praise You for the rest stops along the way called *Grace* and *Mercy*. Sweet sanctuaries to refuel and refresh. I choose to praise You through the journey to Changes."

In a moment's notice, my attitude shifts. A smile emerges. Excitement ignites. The Holy Spirit activates a yearning in my heart. Once again, this phrase resounds, "Life is not about me, but all about Him." Humbleness envelops my soul. I remember 3 John 4… *I have no greater joy than to hear that my children are walking in the Truth.* I am ready, Lord. Ready to journey to Changes!

***

This blog post represented my life in the summer of 2012. God allowed this journey to Changes to be a sweet time of surrender and trust. I praise Him for all He taught me along the way. Entering the empty nest isn't easy, but a necessary and exciting season. To all who have gone before me, "Thank you for the wisdom." For all who follow me, "May you be encouraged to take advantage of every opportunity to teach your children about an intimate relationship with Jesus." The journey to Changes is inevitable.

## LIFE CHALLENGE

Is your life changing? Are you speeding down life's highway without realizing the exit to Changes looms ahead? Are there stops you should have made along the way? Is anxiety building? Maybe you are tired, yet refreshed. Exhausted, yet relieved. Be encouraged and trust God's road signs. The Changes exit causes you to slow down and reflect. Remember, God designed this road map for His glory. Enjoy the journey. With excitement, move forward focusing on God's Word, prayer, and living out His Truths. Ask God to help you follow His road map for your life. And don't miss the rest stops God provides along the way. Give it your all and live sold out for Jesus.

## PRAYER JOURNAL

Read Acts 9 about Paul's experience on the road. Write out a verse that inspires you. Journal your thoughts and prayers.

# ~SILENCE~
# A HIDDEN
# MESSAGE

*And the angel answered and said to him, "I am Gabriel, who stands in the presence of God, and was sent to speak to you and bring you these glad tidings. But behold, you will be mute and not able to speak until the day these things take place, because you did not believe my words which will be fulfilled in their own time."*

—Luke 1:19-20 (NKJV)

Out of silent comes the word listen.

Zacharias, father of John the Baptist, was one of the older priests in his division. God considered Zacharias and his wife, Elizabeth, righteous and blameless because they walked in all the commandments and ordinances of the Lord. In her older age, Elizabeth still desired to be a mother, but she remained a barren woman.

One day while Zacharias was serving the Lord, the lot fell on him to go into the temple to burn the incense. Imagine the scene... He enters the temple to perform an ordinary religious ritual, while outside, the multitudes pray for this normal act of service. While Zacharias is performing his duty, something extraordinary happens —he comes face-to-face with an angel.

What thoughts might have poured into Zacharias' mind? Was he confused? Did he recognize the angel was from God? Let's think beyond the obvious into the heart of Zacharias...

What is going on? Why in the midst of one of my most privileged priesthood duties, am I filled with fear? This must be the angel of death, not the angel of the Lord.

I look into the eyes of the angel as he says, "Do not be afraid, Zacharias. Your prayer has been heard. Your wife, Elizabeth, will bear you a son, and you shall call his name John." What? Elizabeth and I prayed and prayed for God to bless us with a child, but now we are too old. It's impossible for her to become pregnant now.

Doubt surges. Frustration ignites. The angel goes on to say, "He will be filled with the Holy Spirit, even from his mother's womb. And he will turn many of the children of Israel to the Lord their God… to make ready a people prepared for the Lord."

Without thinking I shout, "How shall I know this?" Immediately, remorse fills me. Regret embeds my heart. Looking deep within my soul, the angel of the Lord exclaims, "You will be mute and not able to speak until the day these things take place, because you did not believe my words which will be fulfilled in their own time."

I open my mouth to apologize, but not a word or sound escapes. I try again and again, but nothing. The angel vanishes, and now a heavy burden lies upon my shoulders. Why, in the middle of serving the Lord Most High, did I doubt His answer to our prayers?

Exiting the Temple, I notice the large crowd of people waiting outside. With all my might, I try to share what happened, but I can't utter a sound. Looks of confusion appear on their faces. Whispers ripple through the mob. As my eyes meet Elizabeth's, the words of the angel resound... *Your son will be filled with the Holy Spirit even from birth.*

Frustrated, yet encouraged.
Confused, yet calm.
Fearful, yet humble.

To my surprise, Elizabeth soon conceives a child. Excitement permeates our home. For years we have

151

longed for a baby. My God, our God, has answered our hearts' cries. I open my mouth to shout, "Hallelujah!" But nothing. Not even a whisper escapes. Regret pierces my soul.

In these days of silence, humbleness overwhelms my heart. God's grace, mercy, and love pour upon me. In the quiet, I listen to the voice of the Almighty. A life change stirs deep within my soul. I long to share it with Elizabeth. But how? I trust that in God's timing I will be able to use my voice to explain my transformation.

The day finally arrives. Elizabeth brings forth our son. Relatives and friends rejoice over this miracle baby. Praises to God echo in the valleys and hills, south of Jerusalem. On day eight, when babies are circumcised, the officials ask Elizabeth what name to give the boy. I smile as she boldly says, "John." The authorities begin arguing with her, because no one in our family carried that name. Turning to me they motion for me to write down his name. Instead, I open my mouth and shout, "You are to give him the name John!"

Immediately, I remember Gabriel's words… *You will be mute and not able to speak until the day these things take place, because you did not believe my words, which will be fulfilled in their own time.* Filled with gratitude, I drop to my knees and begin praising God out loud. All in God's perfect timing. Praises release. Humbleness flows. Love pours.

What were the people doing while Zacharias was performing his priestly duties? Praying outside the temple. What a reminder to all of us to pray for our pastors, church staff, ministry leaders, small group leaders, and more. Notice that all of this happened to Zacharias while he was serving the Lord. How many times do we question or doubt God in the midst of serving Him? How often do we allow fear to overtake us?

## LIFE CHALLENGE

Try this little exercise... What other word can you make out of the word SILENT? Hidden in the word silent is the word LISTEN. In many cases, God uses the silent times in our lives to teach us to listen to Him. God used Zacharias' inability to speak, his silence, to teach him a mighty lesson. During this time, Zacharias' attitude changed from doubting to trusting God. Are you experiencing a silent time in your life? Are you listening to the voice of God through His Word? Ask God to help you grow during this difficult season. Through the silent times, live sold out for Jesus.

## PRAYER JOURNAL

Read Luke 1:5-15 and 57-80. What stands out to you in these verses? Journal your thoughts and prayers.

# ~LIFE~
# SHORT CUTS

*It is not good to have zeal without knowledge, nor to be hasty and miss the way.*

—Proverbs 19:2

Take a few minutes to study the photo. Where does this road lead? Why did the driver choose this route? One wrong move, and this automobile could become a real cliffhanger or go tumbling down the mountain. Imagine the driver's physical state... heart beating ninety miles an hour, sweat dripping, hands shaking, and prayers pouring. Can you feel his pain on this road less traveled?

I recall a moment like this in my life. On July 28, 1984, Fred and I married in Abilene, Texas. It was the summer before our senior year at Texas A&M University. Fred was working as an intern for an oil company in Bakersfield, California. After the wedding, we returned to Bakersfield so he could finish his internship. Because we were on a college budget, we decided our honeymoon would be our drive back to Texas. We loaded up our non-air-conditioned 1979 blue Ford pickup, and headed home to the Lone Star State.

Picture this romantic scene... newlyweds riding side-by-side, the windows down, the 120-degree Mojave Desert wind blowing my hair, the smell of perspiration wafting through the air, and the comfort of sleeping in a single cab truck at a roadside park. The perfect setting for a few newlywed spats along the way.

We decided to stop for a couple of days in Red River, New Mexico, for some hiking and relaxation. As I recall, a day into our journey, I was a bit upset because Fred was making all of the decisions. At least that was my opinion. Finally he said, "Okay, you plan our route from Flagstaff, Arizona to Red River, New Mexico." With a sense of confidence and power, I went to work. After unfolding the four-by-four-foot map, I chose the shortest, most direct route. My frustration eased and our romantic honeymoon continued.

I must say I was a bit proud of my chosen route until the paved road turned into a dirt road. Eventually we found ourselves in the middle of an Indian Reservation with no gas stations, rest stops, or convenience stores. To our surprise, this road led straight to a massive cliff overlooking the Royal Gorge. Hot, sweaty, and grumpy, we stepped out of the pickup for a better look. We approached the edge of the cliff, and our mouths dropped open. We realized the only way forward was a very narrow, winding, rocky dirt road twisting its way down the cliff before ending at the river. My thoughts started spinning out of control. We were almost out of gas, so there was no turning back. We started down what seemed more like a path than a road. Fred's hands gripped the steering wheel, holding the truck steady, and we prayed every inch of the way down. We eventually arrived at an old, one lane, wooden bridge, which seemed to serve as a gathering place for teenagers. One after another, they jumped from the bridge into the river. As we slowly traveled over the creaking bridge, the youths stuck their heads in our window and yelled—*Woo, Woo, Woo, Woo!* It felt like we were part of an old western movie.

With huge sighs of relief, we made it to the other side without any problems. Looking back up the cliff, we realized only God could have successfully guided us down this shortcut. We thanked Him for taking care of us and getting us down safely.

I often think back to this frightening life experience. As the decision-maker, I chose the shortest route on the map. I didn't take into account all the obstacles, circumstances, and terrain along the way. What a lesson learned.

God uses real life situations to teach us spiritual life lessons. Do we try to take shortcuts in our Christian lives?

Is God calling us in one direction, but instead we go our own way? The Bible, God's roadmap, serves as our best GPS—God's Positional System. Studying His Word gives us direction, warnings, and insights in how to fully live sold out for Him. God's book of directions leads to a life filled with His love, grace, and mercy.

## LIFE CHALLENGE
Are you heeding God's directions for your life, or going your own way? Do you follow God's roadmap, or do you take short cuts to reach your personal goals. Sticking closely to God's roadmap opens the door for us to understand God's course for our lives. Enjoy the journey. Live sold out for Him. Pray continually. Praise Him in all things.

## PRAYER JOURNAL
Read Genesis 16 with Proverbs 19:2. What shortcut did Sarah take that led to tragedy? Keep in mind, in Genesis 15 God promised Abraham (around age 75) that Sarah (around age 65) would have a son. After ten years of praying for a child with no positive results, Sarah decided to "help God out." What was the result? Write out Proverbs 19:2. Journal your thoughts.

# ~CHOICES~
# DECISION DILEMMA

*Do not fear for I am with you. Do not be dismayed for I am your God. I will strengthen you and help you and uphold you with my righteous right hand.*

—Isaiah 41:10

Doubt. Fear. Decisions.

*Oh Lord, what should I do? I am confused and don't know which way to turn.* Have you experienced these thoughts? Can you recall a time when fear gripped you because of a decision? Personally, when praying about a decision, I would prefer God's answer straight up. A billboard would be nice, or how about an email? Imagine opening your inbox to receive a message from God.

Why doesn't He work this way? As believers, we have the privilege to talk to God twenty-four hours a day, seven days a week. Any time, all the time! He is there waiting to listen, act, and commune with us. He desires an ongoing communication with His children. If you are a parent, you can understand that He doesn't want us to call on Him just during emergencies. Yes, He is there during those times when we need crisis counseling, but He also wants us to come to Him for everyday decisions or concerns.

I remember, as a child, hearing my grandmama pray for parking spots at the grocery store. Sometimes she ended up with a spot close to the front and other times in the boondocks. Regardless of where she ended up parking, she thanked God. She always reminded me that He was in control. In my child's mind, this seemed odd, but the truth she displayed was her ongoing, daily-seeking, trusting, living relationship with Jesus.

A lump still forms in my throat thinking about her, and tears well up. You see, my grandmama showed me what it was like to have a daily connection with Jesus—not a relationship based on what she could *do* for Him, but one based on being *with* Him. I thank God she displayed a living, walking, breathing relationship with Jesus. I praise the Lord for Grandmama and her example of living out a prayerful life. I've often wondered, when I get to heaven will I get to hear a replay of all her prayers over my life?

## LIFE CHALLENGE

When faced with a decision—pray. Pray. PRAY! Whether it's a career change, financial decision, family emergency, child's disciplinary action, relationship issues, or even where to park at the grocery store—pray. Keep a heavenly perspective and watch what God does in and through your life. In the mornings, before your head leaves the pillow, ask God to guide and direct your day. Pray for wisdom and trust Him to lead you. Live sold out for Him through your decision-making process.

## PRAYER JOURNAL

Read Isaiah 41:10 with Proverbs 4. These are powerful verses. Write out the verse that speaks to your heart. Memorize it. Journal your heart's cry.

# ~Unexpected~
# Blockades

*I am the way and the truth and the life. No one comes to the Father except through Me.*

—John 14:6

Do you enjoy making decisions? Have you ever experienced a mind debate? You know, one of those conversations where you try to convince yourself to do one thing over another.

Think about the cereal aisle at the grocery store. A few years ago, selecting a brand of cereal wasn't that difficult.

Now, an overabundance of brands and choices exists. Sometimes I go up and down this aisle saying things like, "This one tastes good, but what about that one? That brand is healthy, but my children like this one better." Are you tracking with me?

Every day we are bombarded with decisions.

Let's do a throwback moment. Do you remember when we didn't have a smartphone or GPS for directions? If you answered yes, then you may have experienced a scenario similar to the following one...

You're late for an event and halfway down the road you remember the directions are on the kitchen table. You kind of recall how to get there, so you decide to keep going. The *so far, so good attitude* keeps you going for a while. But then you approach a fork in the road. Confused, the *I thinks* take over. *I think it's this way. But wait, I think I remember driving by that house.* Now you're driving on instinct, which in many cases leads to driving around in circles. You begin kicking yourself for not going back for the directions.

Choices, choices, choices! Through God's book of directions, the Bible, He teaches us valuable decision-making skills.

Please read Acts 9:1-22. I love dissecting scripture. The Lord always has exciting things for us to learn.

- As a persecutor and collector of the Jews, Paul grew angry toward the followers of Christ—threatening and even murdering some of them. His persecution toward believers was becoming more and more intense. Jesus became Paul's roadblock. Why? So that Paul's eyes would be opened to the truth and message of Jesus. God's plan to use Paul for His glory came at the perfect time. (Acts 9:15)

- Focus on Acts 9:2 and compare it to John 14:6. Notice, the phrase *the way* is used in both verses. Here, the Greek for the root word *way*, is *hodos*. It means a traveler's way, journey, a traveled road, or road.[8] Isn't it interesting how God works? This same phrase, *the Way*, which Paul used to describe followers of Christ is the same word Jesus used to describe Himself... *I am the way, the truth, and the life (John 14:6)*. Ironically, Jesus met Paul on a well-traveled road, while Paul, a collector of Jews, journeyed to arrest any who were of *the Way*.

- In Acts 9:11, I find it interesting that Jesus sends Paul (Saul) to Straight Street in Damascus. The Greek word for *straight* is *euthus*, which means straightforward, upright, true, and sincere.[9] *The Way*, Jesus, needed Paul to have a straight and clear understanding that He is God's son, sent by God to save the world. He is the Redeemer, God in the flesh, the Messiah, King of kings, and Lord of lords.

Do you remember a time when you traveled down the wrong road? How did Jesus halt you on your journey and point you to the right way? At the time, did you realize Jesus was rerouting you to Straight Street?

## LIFE CHALLENGE

As we journey through life, we find many opportunities to take a wrong turn. These side roads may lead in the wrong direction or take us the long way around to our destination. However, when we follow God's roadmap (the Bible), we travel the way of the Master Designer's plan, and in many cases it helps us avoid rough roads, potholes, and broken bridges. Look at life's roadblocks or barricades as God's way of redirecting you. Focusing on Jesus keeps your heart and mind centered on His purposes.

## PRAYER JOURNAL

Read all of Acts 9:1-22. What stands out to you in these verses? Journal your thoughts and prayers.

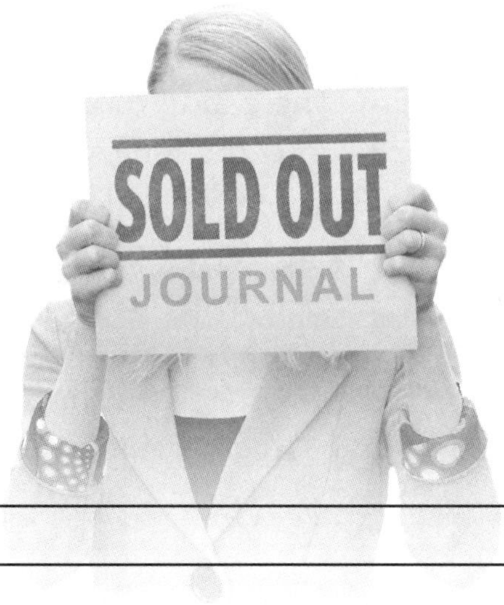
SOLD OUT
JOURNAL

# CHAPTER 7
# REFILL YOUR HOPE

*Praise be to the God and Father of our Lord Jesus Christ! In his great mercy He has given us new birth into a living **hope** through the resurrection of Jesus Christ from the dead, and into an inheritance that can never perish, spoil or fade - kept in heaven for you, who through faith are shielded by God's power until the coming of the salvation that is ready to be revealed in the last time.*

—1 Peter 1:3-5

I hope he gets the job. I hope they move to another house. I hope you feel better.

Where is the emphasis in these statements? On the person making the comment or on whomever the comment is about? It's on the person talking. In many cases, we use the word *hope* to emphasize a feeling or human desire.[10] This is quite different from the *hope* Peter is declaring in 1 Peter 1:3-5.

Today we use the word *hope* to describe our ambitions, wishes, and desires. When looking at the original Greek language, however, the word has quite a different meaning. The Greek word for hope is *elpis,* which means joyful and confident expectation of eternal salvation.[11] It's used to portray blissfulness, joyfulness, and assurance of eternal salvation. The English definition focuses on satisfying human desires. The Greek focuses on a *hope* that goes beyond a moment in time, a *hope* that is everlasting.

The sections in *Refill Your Hope* focus on living day to day with a heavenly perspective rather than an earthly point of view. Expect splashes of encouragement throughout this chapter. Ask the Holy Spirit to reveal truth and understanding as you read each entry. Look for these themes...

- Find hope in Jesus, not circumstances.
- Desire to live a life empowered by the Holy Spirit through Jesus.
- Crave to seek the Lord's truth for spiritual nourishment.

- Build your life on Jesus, the Cornerstone.

- Be living stones, empowered by Jesus.

Chapters 7 and 8 lead us through 1 Peter—a book written to encourage Christians during difficult times. Throughout this book, Peter emphasizes that we should expect suffering and heartache in our lives. His powerful words lead us to understand how God uses suffering to shape our character and make us more like Christ. May the Lord bless you through this journey of 1 Peter.

# ~TRUST~
# A ROOM WITH
# A VIEW

*In this you greatly rejoice, though for a little while you may have had to suffer grief in all kinds of trials. These have come so that your faith—of greater worth than gold, which perishes even though refined by fire, may be proved genuine and may result in praise, glory and honor when Jesus Christ is revealed.*
—1 Peter 1:6-7

Fresh air. Breath-taking view. Open Bible. Just breathing ignites a smile. God's Word brings my heart and soul into oneness with Jesus through the Holy Spirit. Glancing down at my Bible, I read Peter 1:3-5...

*Praise be to the God and Father of our Lord Jesus Christ! In his great mercy He has given us new birth into a living* **hope** *through the resurrection of Jesus Christ from the dead, and into an inheritance that can never perish, spoil or fade - kept in heaven for you, who through faith are shielded by God's power until the coming of the salvation that is ready to be revealed in the last time.*

Praises flow. Humbleness pours. Heart warms. Scanning the tops of the mountains brings warmth. In the distance, a dark cloud begins to creep over the peaks and into the valleys. Frustration surfaces. The beauty eventually fades into the haze. Faced with a choice, to walk away or trust the view will return—I choose to wait.

All at once, a gentle breeze rustles the tattered pages of my Bible. 1 Peter 1:6-7 comes into focus...

*In this you greatly rejoice, though for a little while you may have had to suffer grief in all kinds of trials. These have come so that your faith—of greater worth than gold, which perishes even though refined by fire, may be proved genuine and may result in praise, glory and honor when Jesus Christ is revealed.*

God's voice resonates. In a moment's notice, this room with a view presents itself as God's spiritual life lesson. Like a light illuminating its surroundings, understanding penetrates my soul. For a time, the heavy haze veils this majestic scene. Trusting that the dark cloud will lift is crucial. The same is true with believers in Jesus. We must base our living hope in Jesus, not on our circumstances. God allows life situations to strengthen our faith and trust in Him.

Our family recently enjoyed a vacation in Belize. One afternoon, we stopped at a beachfront café for lunch. The beauty surrounding us filled our hearts with peace. After placing our order, we waited patiently for the food to arrive. While waiting, we watched dolphins play in the waves, seagulls dive for their lunch, and people stroll along the shoreline. After an hour and a half, we wondered why our food hadn't arrived. Finally, I walked up to the counter and asked our young waiter what was taking so long. With a slight hesitation he responded, "Ma'am, please accept my apology. I forgot to turn in your order." All of a sudden, a haze of frustration settled in. Faced with a choice to either verbally abuse our waiter or accept his apology, I inwardly prayed, "God, how should I respond? Please give me the words to say." Trusting the prompting of the Holy Spirit, I motioned to our table and said, "Just like Jesus granted us grace and forgiveness, so we, as His children, give grace and forgiveness to you." Immediately, tears welled up in his eyes. He grabbed my hand saying, "Thank you so much! Blessings to you."

God used this situation to teach us a spiritual life lesson. If we allowed this irritating incident to cloud our view, we would have missed the beauty of a divine appointment. God opened the door for us to practice patience, forgiveness, and grace. Trusting God was crucial to seeing past our room with a view.

## LIFE CHALLENGE

Are you experiencing a room with a view? Is the scene hopeful or disappointing? Looking past the obvious allows God to show us His spiritual life lessons. Trust Peter's words. He speaks truth. The dark cloud will soon pass. Don't miss the opportunity to deepen your faith in Jesus through your room with a view. Live sold out for Him. Remember... *In his great mercy He has given us new birth into a living hope through the resurrection of Jesus Christ from the dead, and into an inheritance that can never perish, spoil or fade—kept in heaven for you.*

—1 Peter 1:3-4

## PRAYER JOURNAL

Read 1 Peter 1:1-12. Write out your favorite verse from this block of scripture. Journal your thoughts.

# ~THE CROSS~
# REDEEMED

*For you know that it was not with perishable things such as silver or gold that you were redeemed from the empty way of life handed down to you from your forefathers, but with the precious blood of Christ, a lamb without blemish or defect.*

—1 Peter 1:18, 19

Do you live for Him? Do you live with a heavenly perspective or an earthly point of view? Think for a moment. Be honest. Where is your focus—the world or Jesus?

Embedded in the midst of 1 Peter 1:18 is the word *redeemed*. Redeemed from what? Redeemed by whom? Redeemed why? What is God saying to us?

*Redeemed* carries a deep meaning—to be released from one's self by payment of a ransom. Moreover, *redeemed* means to be delivered from every kind of evil, whether internal or external. The redeemed one is the receiver. The one who pays the ransom is the giver. Redemption is an unmerited gift filled with grace, love, and mercy. An unconditional love offering with no strings attached.

Tears well up. Humbleness dwells in my heart. Jesus paid it all. He exchanged Himself for our ransom—my ransom. He rescued all who trust in Him from the penalty of sin. Jesus bridged the gap between God and us. Not because we deserved it, but because He loved us.

Questions arise, "How do I live for Him? How do I live reflecting God's abundant love, grace, and mercy?" Perhaps the following acronym will help you reflect and remember ways to keep a heavenly perspective.

## REDEEM...

<u>RE</u>-new:

Living for Him is a choice. Renewing our hearts through God's Word and prayer helps us see who we are in

Christ—redeemed. Make a decision to call upon Him every day. Renew your strength in Him. Refresh your mind by realizing Jesus redeemed you and paid the penalty for your sin.

<u>DE</u>-sire:

Desiring to live every moment for Jesus changes our attitudes. Reminding ourselves of Jesus' sacrifice and love on the cross keeps us focused on Him. God knows the desires of our hearts. He knows whether we serve Him out of selfish gain or to further the Kingdom of God. Desire to seek Jesus first. I love how my daddy prays, "Jesus, I love you and just want to love you more." Thanks, Dad, for those simple, yet powerful words!

<u>EM</u>-power:

The Holy Spirit, Jesus' Spirit, empowers us to trust, respond, and follow God's Word. We can't create this internal power ourselves. This is the Holy Spirit's job. Romans 15:17-19 states, *Therefore, I glory in Christ Jesus in my service to God. I will not venture to speak of anything except what Christ has accomplished through me in leading the Gentiles to obey God by what I have said and done—by the power of signs and miracles, through the power of the Spirit.* By surrendering and allowing the Holy Spirit to empower us with the gifts of the Spirit (Galatians 3:22), we become empty of ourselves and filled with the Spirit.

## LIFE CHALLENGE

Renew your desire to live a life empowered by the Holy Spirit through Jesus. Remember, "Life is not about me, but all about Him." Living every moment knowing you are redeemed by the blood of Jesus changes your perspective on decisions, actions, and circumstances. Praise God for His grace and mercy, which go beyond our understanding. Never forget—our hope is in Jesus, our Redeemer forever.

## PRAYER JOURNAL

Read 1 Peter 1:13-25. Which verse stands out? Write it down. Memorize it. Journal your thoughts and prayers.

# ~THE WORD~
# SPIRITUAL
# NOURISHMENT

*Therefore, rid yourselves of all malice and all deceit, hypocrisy, envy, and all slander of every kind. Like newborn babies, crave pure spiritual milk, so that by it you may grow up in your salvation.*

—1 Peter 2:1-2

I love dissecting scripture. Grasping the true meaning of the words from the Greek and Hebrew definitions provides spiritual nourishment to my soul. It's like examining the nutritional facts on the sides of food boxes. It gives understanding and clarity to what I'm about to ingest.

Get ready for a fun journey as we dig into 1 Peter 2:1-2. These verses focus on eliminating fleshly desires from our lives. It's easy to pass over this verse or put a mark by it as if to say, "I can check this one off my list. I'm not a malicious or dishonest person. I live my life for Jesus and I don't envy others. I don't…" However, in the blink of an eye, thoughts arise… *If only I could take back the words I said about my neighbor. Why did I speak to my children with that tone of voice?* Reality surfaces. Confession opens the door to a clean conscience.

God gives us a real life analogy for a spiritual life lesson through 1 Peter 2:2. *Like newborn babies, crave pure spiritual milk, so that by it you may grow up in your salvation.*

*Crave:* to desire, or pursue with love, and to long after.[12]

*Pure:* unmixed, unadulterated, or sincere.[13]

*Milk*: metaphor for the simpler or fundamental truths in God's Word.[14]

What do you long for in life? Do you crave more money, success, power, recognition, material things, or possibly perfection? Or do you desire righteousness, mercy, and grace through Jesus? God calls us to *be transformed into His likeness with ever-increasing glory, which comes from the Lord.* (2 Corinthians 3:18)

Would you mix a teaspoon of garlic in a bottle of milk for your baby? No way! His little tummy would be upset for hours. Neither is it a good idea to water down your baby's milk to the point of depleting the nutrients.

Just as an infant requires pure milk, our walk with Jesus must contain purified, unpolluted, sincere biblical truths. The result—spiritual nourishment.

More than likely, you have heard the statement, "You are what you eat." There are even book titles containing this phrase. These books focus on nutritional programs to improve health and change dietary habits. I see a spiritual life lesson forming!

Just as healthy physical food energizes the physical body, so feeding on the true and solid Word of God feeds the soul. Now we are getting somewhere! In order to grow in our walk with the Lord and experience spiritual nourishment, we must first desire the sincere and unaltered truths of God's Word.

As we humbly crave and grasp the gift of God's grace and unconditional love through His son, Jesus, our souls are nourished. Take hold of the phrase, "Life is not about me, but all about Him." Let it sink in and make it your own.

## LIFE CHALLENGE

Our hope is in the God of Truth. Can a baby survive on one bottle of milk a week? No. It's more like six to eight bottles a day. Likewise, can a child of God grow and mature spiritually with just one feeding on Sunday mornings? Our Christian lives would be weak and frail. This week, crave to seek the Lord's truths through reading His Word, praying throughout your day, and looking for God's life lessons along the way. He is waiting to give you spiritual nourishment!

## PRAYER JOURNAL

Read and write out 1 Peter 2:1-3. Journal what God is teaching you through these verses.

# ~BUILDING~
# LIVING STONES

*As you come to Him, the living Stone—rejected by men but chosen by God and precious to Him—you also, like **living stones**, are being built into a spiritual house to be a holy priesthood.*

—1 Peter 2:4-5

Jesus' arrest. His trial. His crucifixion. His death. His burial. His resurrection.

Realizing Jesus took on the sins of all mankind and conquered Satan forever brings me to my knees. Praises flow. Gratefulness floods my soul.

As I read 1 Peter 2:4-5, the phrases *the living Stone* and *living stones,* seem to bounce off the page. Immediately, my thoughts turn to Jesus' tomb. *So Joseph bought some linen cloth, took down the body, wrapped Him in the linen, and he placed Him in a tomb cut out of the **rock**, and rolled a **stone** against the door of the tomb.* (Mark 15:46)

To grasp the fullness of these phrases let's do a little background work...

- *Rock:* metaphor for a man - like a rock, with firmness and strength of the soul[15]
- *Stone:* metaphor for Christ - like building stones[16]
- *Living:* to be in full vigor, to be fresh, strong, efficient, active, powerful[17]

After His crucifixion, Jesus was placed inside a cold, dark, hollowed-out rock. For security reasons, a heavy stone was placed at the opening of the tomb. No way in, no way out. It's at this point we almost hear a crescendo playing in the heavens.

What were the disciples feeling at this point? Defeat, guilt, anger, doubt, embarrassment, confusion, bewilderment? Maybe the stone represented a spiritual closure in their own lives. Like a light fading into the darkness, their hope vanished into the darkness of despair. The following days must have felt like a lifetime.

Three days after Jesus' death, early in the morning, a group of women visited the burial site. Possibly on their way, they discussed ways to remove the heavy stone from the entrance. To their amazement, when they arrived, the stone was already rolled away!

Morning sunlight now illuminated the once dark and gloomy vault. The grave overflowed with the light of Christ. Nothing could prevent God from carrying out his ultimate plan. Not a lifeless stone. Not Satan and his army. Jesus is alive! *The living Stone—rejected by men but chosen by God.*

As followers of *the living Stone*, we are charged with the same purpose—to be *living stones*. Dead rocks are worthless because they do not contain energy. But *living stones* bring freshness, full vigor, and strength. Believers who are living stones are efficient, active, and have the power to build spiritual houses.

## LIFE CHALLENGE

Our hope is in Jesus. He is alive! Jesus is *the living Stone*—our living Stone. He calls us to build our lives on Him, the solid Rock. Peter refers to all believers in Jesus as *living stones*. God's plan is for His children to work together to build His Kingdom. Remember to thank God for the *living stones* He has placed in your life. Relish each one as a vital part of the building process. Allow God to use others to help you live sold out for Jesus.

## PRAYER JOURNAL
Read 1 Peter 2:4-12. Which verse stands out to you? Write it out. Praise God for the *living stones* in your life.

# ~THE SOLID ROCK~
# A PRECIOUS STONE

*Therefore, to you who believe, He is precious; but to those who are disobedient, "The Stone which the builders rejected has become the Chief Cornerstone.*

—1 Peter 2:7 (NJKV)

How would you describe the word *precious*? Expensive, rare, valuable, costly, prized, shiny? These descriptions may explain today's meaning of *precious*, but what is Peter conveying to the reader?

As a reminder, *stone* in the Greek language is a metaphor for Christ—like building stones.[18] *Precious* in the Greek means fixed value on the price, the payment of a price, payment received for a person or thing bought or sold.[19]

Jesus, *the precious Stone*, paid the fixed price for our sins through His death on the cross. Reflecting on this truth produces a humble heart. Our salvation comes through Jesus, bought and sold with His blood. Tears emerge. Praises release. "Thank you, God, for sending Your Son as payment—past, present, and future."

I can hardly get past this truth. God doesn't require a checklist of dos and don'ts to be accepted by Him. My salvation doesn't depend on my behavior. Salvation is given in the form of a gift called *grace*. God sent His Son, Jesus, who gave His life in exchange for ours when He died and rose again. He is our redeemer. He gives eternal hope to all who believe in Jesus. Forever and ever! Amen.

Think back to 1 Peter 2:7. What is the meaning of the *Chief Cornerstone*? The Greek word for *cornerstone* is *gonia*, which means an external angle or corner of a building[20] like a keystone or anchor. In ancient construction, the chief cornerstone was the first stone placed in the building's foundation. All the other stones were aligned to this main stone. Without the proper placement, the building might be unstable, shift, and over time crumble to the ground.

The same is true of our spiritual walk. Building our lives on Jesus, *the Chief Cornerstone*, gives us firm spiritual foundations, which won't crumble when the wind blows, the earth shakes, or the storms of life rage. Jesus is the only one who brings stability to a person, family, or nation.

## LIFE CHALLENGE

Our hope is in Jesus—the solid Rock, *the precious Stone*. Are you aligning your spiritual home to the *Chief Cornerstone*? Or, are you stacking your stones and then trying to fit Jesus into your construction? Remember, God's architectural design centers on the *Chief Cornerstone*. The more we read the plan book, the more we understand that Jesus is the only solid Stone equipped to handle the pressures in our lives. Take time to examine your spiritual building project. Precious Jesus is ready and waiting to be placed first in your life. Remember, He gave His life to save yours. Enjoy the construction process!

## PRAYER JOURNAL

Read 1 Peter 2: 1-10. Write out the verse that stirs your heart. Journal a prayer that represents what you are feeling right now. You are precious to Him.

# CHAPTER 8

# READY YOUR WALK

*I say then: Walk in the Spirit, and you shall not fulfill the lust of the flesh. For the flesh lusts against the Spirit, and the Spirit against the flesh; and these are contrary to one another, so that you do not do the things that you wish.*

—Galatians 5:16-17 (NKJV)

What does it mean to *walk in the Spirit*? Is Paul, the writer of Galatians, focusing on the physical act of walking down the street? Or is there something more to this phrase? Digging deeper into the Bible's original text, we find the answers to our questions.

Did you know the word *walk* is used over and over throughout God's Word? The Greek word for *walk* in the New Testament is *peripateo* which means to walk, to make one's way, progress; make due use of opportunities.[21] *Walk* also gives the idea of a continuous mode of conduct or behavior. In fact, the related verb form *to walk* comes from the Hebrew definition of the phrase *to live,* which means to regulate one's life, conduct oneself.[22]

In other words, *walk in the Spirit* could be correctly translated as *to live by the Spirit.* Learning to live moment-by-moment for Jesus is the ultimate purpose for this book—*Sold Out: Live for Him.*

Prepare yourself to ready the walk through these next five entries. Before reading, pray. Ask the Holy Spirit to bring revelation to your heart and mind. Ask Him to shed light on the scriptures you read. Look for these themes…

- God's purposes as you walk through life
- God's ways as you walk in your marriage
- God's divine appointments throughout your day
- How God's Word steadies our walk
- How God's love stabilizes our walk as we cast our cares on Him

Sit back. Take a deep breath. Begin this week's lesson with a heart that says, "I am ready to walk in the Light of Christ—in my heart, actions, and attitude." May the Lord reveal His love for you in tender and sweet ways.

# ~GOD'S PURPOSES~ JUST FOR THE UNJUST

*For it is commendable if a man bears up under the pain of unjust suffering because he is conscious of God. But how is it to your credit if you receive a beating for doing wrong and endure it? But if you suffer for doing good and you endure it, this is commendable before God.*

—1 Peter 2:19-20

For a brief moment, I felt I was in the presence of a modern day Paul. A lump slowly formed in my throat. In silence, I praised the Lord for allowing me the opportunity to meet a man who said, "Life's not fair. And it's not supposed to be. We are not on this earth for our glory, but for God's glory." With grace, these words gently flowed from the missionary's mouth.

On a short-term mission trip to Haiti, our group of nine spent an evening with a missionary couple. This couple serves in their community by feeding the homeless, helping the needy, and loving the motherless. In fact, they adopted more than twenty children into their family. Their home was filled with so much love, tenderness, and incredible organization!

A few years ago this godly man was arrested and held in a Haitian jail for months. Why? There is still no clear answer. No charges were ever filed against him.

During his imprisonment, he experienced unsanitary conditions, unfair treatment, disease-infested quarters, and sharing a 10x12 cell with multiple inmates. He watched many die from tuberculosis and cholera outbreaks.

Silence filled the room as he told his story. Our team was speechless. Thoughts poured in like... *How unfair! How unjust!*

This couple was in the Lord's service, loving the Haitian people, helping the fatherless, embracing the motherless, feeding the hungry, and clothing the needy. My blood began to boil when this thought poured in—*Lord, why would you allow this to happen to them?* As quickly as the question popped into my mind, the Holy Spirit countered it with this truth—*What Satan means for evil, God uses for good to those who allow Him to use their story, for His glory!*

At this point, I started listening to my new friend with an open heart. His tone and body language showed no signs of bitterness, vengeance, or need for retaliation. The Fruit of the Spirit flowed through him in a way I've never seen before—love, joy, peace, patience, kindness, goodness, gentleness, faithfulness, and self-control. These words suddenly shot out of my mouth… "How do you forgive all those who treated you this way? What are you doing with the anger and pain?" He looked at me and calmly replied…

"I don't have it in me to forgive or let go of these unfair acts my family was forced to endure. It's only through God's grace and mercy that I was able to let go of my anger. God performed a real miracle in my heart. Anything you see in me has come from Jesus. Because of what happened to me, God opened the door to a new prison ministry. Now the guards are my good friends. I visit with the inmates on a regular basis, providing them with medicines, food, Bibles, and God's love. You see, I understand what they are experiencing and know how to minister to them in a way I wouldn't have known before."

Humbleness engulfed me. God bumps ignited. Even now, years later, this conversation remains fresh in my mind. I am changed because one man made the decision to live his life sold out for Jesus.

## LIFE CHALLENGE

This missionary's statement is a challenge for all of us—
*Life's not fair. And it's not supposed to be fair. We are not on
this earth for our glory, but for God's glory.* Jesus endured
the cross—guiltless. Paul encountered imprisonment—
blameless. So, when life isn't fair, embrace the moment.
Look for His purposes in the unjust situations and allow
God to use them for His glory. Like my friend, live sold
out for Jesus.

## PRAYER JOURNAL

Read 1 Peter 2:13-25 with 1 Peter 4:12-19. Which verse
captures your heart? Write it out. Journal your thoughts.

# ~GOD'S WAYS~
# MARRIAGE BLISS

*Wives, in the same way **submit** to your own husbands so that, if any of them do not believe the Word, they may be won over without words by the behavior of their wives, when they see the purity and reverence of your lives. Husbands, in the same way, be **considerate** as you live with your wives, and treat them with respect as the weaker partner and as heirs with you of the gracious gift of life, so that nothing will hinder your prayers.*

—1 Peter 3:1-2, 7

Consider the following words within the context of the wife's role... submit, submissive, and submission.

What thoughts arise when you read these words? Doormat, bondage, controlling? Possibly your reaction stems from the world's ideas, "No one's going to tell me what to do. I am my own person. I can make my own choices." What does God really mean when He uses the word *submissive*?

Now, consider the following words within the context of the husband's role... considerate, thoughtful, and tactful.

How do you compare this series of words to the previous list? In a more positive way? Why? What makes this word list different from the first group? Could it be because of the way we commonly use these words in today's culture?

Let's do a little investigating or what I like to call Scripture Excavation. You just might change the way you view the word *submit*. Look at scripture excavation as a way to find the keys to unlocking the mysteries within God's Word.

*Submit* or *submissive*, in the Greek, is *hypotasso*, which means yielding to one's admonition or advice, to be subject to another, a conscious choice to voluntarily unite, to cooperate, to relinquish control.[23] In this definition, do you see anything about acting as a doormat or being controlled by someone else? No, not at all! *Submit* was a Greek militant term used to organize troops in a combat order under the command of a leader.[24]

We just uncovered one of the keys to unlocking what God is telling us about *submission* in His Word. As Christians, we should surrender or submit our lives to Jesus. We need to voluntarily relinquish control and come under His authority. As the husband surrenders to Christ, God calls him to spiritually lead his family. God's plan is set for the wife to voluntarily come under her husband's leadership. Notice, this is not a dictated position, but a choice that is covered by God's umbrella of protection of love, grace, and mercy.

God directs the wife to yield to her husband's leadership, direction, and authority. I love that Peter doesn't stop with the wife's responsibilities. He ends with how the husband is to conduct himself. The husband is to be *considerate* and treat his wife with respect. Digging into the actual meaning of the word *considerate*, we find another hidden key. Going back to the Greek, the word *gnosis* is used. It means a deeper, more perfect, and enlarged knowledge of the Christian religion, moral wisdom – such as living right.[25]

The husband is called to help his wife gain a better understanding of God's Word, to lead her to a deeper walk with Jesus, and to respect her.

Read today's scripture one more time. Notice how the phrase *in the same way* is used when Peter addresses the husband **and** the wife. They are both required to participate equally in the marriage covenant. We could even substitute *likewise* for the phrase *in the same way*. It truly is a full circle process. The wife submits. The husband spiritually leads with respect... *So that nothing will hinder your prayers.*

How exciting! God loves us enough to give us marriage guidelines. By focusing on God's ways and not the world's ideas, we understand our part in God's plan for marriage. God blesses those who submit to His instructions.

## LIFE CHALLENGE

Wives, is pride halting you from submitting to your husband? Husbands, are you failing to lead your wife in a deeper walk with Jesus? Are your prayers hindered because of neglect or misunderstanding of your role as a wife or husband? Ask the Lord to help you submit to Him and follow His guidelines for marriage. Be prepared for what God shows you. Enjoy living sold out for Him in and through your marriage.

## PRAYER JOURNAL

Read 1 Peter 3:1-7 with Ephesians 5:22-33. Which verse applies to your life or marriage role? Write it out. Memorize it. Journal your thoughts.

# ~GOD'S PROVISION~
# READY?

*Who is going to harm you if you are eager to do good? But even if you should suffer for what is right, you are blessed. "Do not fear what they fear; do not be frightened." But in your hearts set apart Christ as Lord. Always be prepared to give an answer to everyone who asks you to give the reason for the hope that you have. But do this with gentleness and respect, keeping a clear conscience, so that those who speak maliciously against your good behavior in Christ may be ashamed of their slander.*

*It is better, if it is God's will, to suffer for doing good than for doing evil.*

—1 Peter 3:13-17

Are you ready? What are you ready for—work, shopping, vacation, dinner, the weekend, or your everyday activities? Are you anticipating a move, the birth of a child, the death of a loved one, the empty nest, or just a change in the weather? Life constantly changes. Planning is an essential part of the process.

You may think you're ready, but are you *really?* Are you ready for God's divine appointments? Are you prepared to love and serve Jesus with all your heart, soul, mind and strength, even when you don't feel like it? Are you ready to give God the glory, rather than take it for yourself? Ask God to prepare you to live sold out for Him.

One morning after time in my prayer chair, I prepared my to-do list. A sigh escaped as I reviewed my agenda. A prayer released, "Lord, let this day be yours. With so little time, I'm not sure how I can complete this list. I give it to You. Help me experience You in the midst of my day. Amen."

This prayer changed my perspective. My day's schedule consisted of errands like going to the grocery store, the dry cleaners, shopping for shoes, and making other routine stops. About halfway through the checklist, God reminded me again, "Remember, My child, this is My agenda for you." Still in the "I can do it" mode, I forged ahead. Until… I literally bumped into a lady at the shoe store. We smiled and said our apologies. Then, as if looking into my soul, she said, "The Spirit of Jesus shines on your face." Immediately our hearts united. During our brief conversation, she shared the news she'd received that morning about her cancer diagnosis. I asked if I could pray for her, and the moment became forever embedded in my heart. "Thank You, Lord, for teaching me to be ready and prepared for Your daily assignments in the middle of my routines. Amen."

I love 1 Peter 3:15… *But in your hearts set apart Christ as Lord. Always be prepared to give an answer to everyone who asks you to give the reason for the hope that you have.* A believer's answer to the question, "Are you ready?" should always be, "YES!" We are living, breathing testimonies of a new creation in Jesus. To live for Him should be our heart's desire. Recognizing it is not about us, but all about Him, changes us, and in turn affects others around us.

So how do we live out this verse? Here are three suggestions:

- **Pray**—Stay intimately connected to the Lord. Prayer keeps our hearts tuned to Jesus. Learning to live in constant communication with God readies us for what lies ahead.

- **Observe**—Keep your eyes open to God's divine appointments. Through these opportunities, God enables you to share the truth and message of Jesus.

- **Act**—Step up and share Jesus with others. When God opens a door, trust Him. He has already prepared the way.

## LIFE CHALLENGE

Are you ready? Look for the opportunities He brings your way. Then with excitement, put into action the plans He gives you to share with others. Serving Jesus is so much fun! Live sold out for Him.

## PRAYER JOURNAL

Read 1 Peter 3:8-22. Write out the verse that touches your heart. Journal a prayer of praise.

# ~GOD'S WORD~
# WHEN GOD
# SPEAKS—LISTEN

*If anyone speaks, he should do it as one speaking the very words of God. If anyone serves, he should do it with the strength God provides, so that in all things God may be praised through Jesus Christ. To Him be the glory and power forever and ever. Amen.*
—1 Peter 4:11

When God speaks—listen.

Reading God's Word is so much fun! Have you ever read a verse and like springtime bursting into bloom, the scripture comes alive in your heart and mind? It may be a verse you've read over and over, but for some reason, at that moment, it takes on a fresh meaning in your life. It truly is amazing! The Holy Spirit connects our minds, hearts, and souls to Jesus as we learn God's Truths through His Word. As a result, I find...

The more I read God's Word, the more I know Him.

The more I know Him, the more I love Him.

The more I love Him, the more I crave Him.

The more I crave Him, the more I live for Him.

One morning a few years back, I was settled into my prayer chair with my first cup of coffee, my five-pound Maltese at my side and my Bible in hand. I was armed and ready for my quiet time. For some odd reason, I veered away from my usual devotional series, and decided to play the Bible bingo game. You know, the "what should I read this morning" method. He directed me to 1 Peter 4:11. The words jumped off the page and into my heart...

*If anyone speaks, he should do it as one speaking the very words of God. If anyone serves, he should do it with the strength God provides, so that in all things God may be praised through Jesus Christ.*

—1 Peter 4:11

Immediately, the Holy Spirit pulled at my heartstrings as these powerful words filled me with a fresh perspective. A gentle, yet powerful voice echoed in my heart and soul...

"This is your life verse for the year. Memorize it. Believe it. Live it!"

I quickly responded with, "God, what does a life verse mean? What are you saying to me?" Again, I felt the Lord say to me...

"Carla, My daughter, every time you open your mouth, let My words flow. When you serve as a wife and mother or in ministry through Reflective Life Ministries, let it always be through the strength that I give you. Never in your power! So in all things I will be glorified through your relationship with My Son, Jesus! I am giving you this verse to live by for the year. Claim it. Apply it. Live it!"

I followed the prompting of the Holy Spirit and claimed 1 Peter 4:11 as my focus verse that year. Glory to God! He used this verse to remind me to always live sold out for Jesus in everything I say and do and to serve in the strength He gives. It humbles me to realize His love goes beyond my understanding.

## LIFE CHALLENGE

When God speaks—listen. Ask the Lord to show you a focus verse. It is so exciting to see what He reveals. Write it out. Memorize it. Place it in a strategic area—on your bathroom mirror, in your car, on the computer, on the coffee pot. Have fun as the Lord directs you. Share this idea with other people. You never know how something the Lord reveals to you might benefit others.

## PRAYER JOURNAL

Read 1 Peter 4. What verse touches your heart? Be still. Listen for God's whisper. What is He saying? Write it down.

# ~GOD'S CARE~
# CAST IT ALL

*Humble yourselves, therefore, under God's mighty hand, that He may lift you up in due time. Cast all your anxiety on him because He cares for you.*

—1 Peter 5:6

Sleeping late, going swimming, taking family vacations, playing with friends, catching fireflies. School is out for the summer!

Imagine all of the students staring at the clock on the wall and counting down the last seconds of the school year. The moment the bell sounds, a sense of freedom explodes—freedom from homework, school schedules, peer pressure, and teachers. Cheers echo through the hallways. Joy fills the building.

While children anticipate the excitement of summer break, moms wonder what the summer holds. Do you know what I mean?

The summer of 1998 was a life-changer in the McDougal house. On the last day of school, our four children, ages twelve and under, ran into the house, screaming, "SCHOOL IS OUT! SCHOOL IS OUT!" Thoughts flooded my mind. What are we going to do for the next three months? How am I going to keep them from fighting? All of a sudden, another thought popped in, I know what to do. I'll keep them involved in swim lessons, t-ball, dance, piano, science camp, playgroups, and Vacation Bible School. Excitedly, I forged ahead with my plans, creating an organizational spreadsheet filled with weekly activities.

During the first part of the summer, busyness consumed our lives. As a result, stress levels increased, creating anxiety and discontent in the whole family. Little did I know, out of my desire for a trouble-free summer, I was watering seeds of selfishness and self-focus in my children. Sadly, the very things I worried about were being nurtured. Then one day during my quiet time, God captured my heart. He seemed to say, "Carla, you love your children, and I know you desire for them to seek Me with all their hearts. But you are creating an atmosphere focused on things and busyness. Your children are slowly developing a 'life is all about me' attitude. Now is the time to make changes." God led me to Isaiah 54:13 (NKJV)...

*All your children shall be taught by the Lord, and great shall be the peace of your children.*

Immediately, the phrase... and great shall be the peace of your children resonated within my soul. I sensed God saying, "Here is your answer to a peaceful summer. I'm not saying perfect, but peaceful." I was convicted to give my anxiety to Jesus. To my surprise, in an instant, calmness flowed over me. Confessions streamed. Freshness penetrated my soul. Praises burst from my mouth.

I completely adjusted the final weeks of our summer schedule. This change allowed us to center on serving, rather than receiving. Giving, rather than taking. We replaced activities that separated the family with activities that brought us together. We focused more on living out God's Word in our family. This resulted in an attitude adjustment for all of us.

God used this experience to teach me a lifelong lesson... to cast ALL of my burdens and cares upon Him. I have to admit, this takes practice, and I can't accomplish it on my own. It's the power of the Holy Spirit working in and through me, reminding me to surrender everything to Jesus. As the old saying goes, "Over time, practice becomes a habit." When I practice giving every thought, action, and even my daily schedule over to the Lord, He begins to change my perspective and outlook about my day. And, guess what? I can NEVER get the glory. He receives the glory and honor for it all. Amen.

*"The chains of habit are too weak to be felt until they are too strong to be broken."*

—Samuel Johnson

## LIFE CHALLENGE

Are you anticipating a change or decision that may affect your life situation? Ask the Lord to help you stay focused on Jesus. Cast all your cares upon Him—even your mommy burdens. Take to heart Isaiah 54:13. Be your children's example of surrendering it all to Jesus when playing games, driving in the car, cooking for the family, disciplining them, praying with them, serving others, and setting the family schedule. If you are a grandparent, let the light of Christ shine through you. What a gift God gives us to pass the love of Jesus to the next generation.

## PRAYER JOURNAL

Read 1 Peter 5. Focus on verse 6. What do you learn from this verse? After completing 1 Peter, journal what God taught you through Peter's heart. Let this truth resonate within your soul. Ask God to help you move it from head knowledge, to heart knowledge, to actions in your life, as you live sold out for Jesus.

# FROM MY HEART

*For to me, to live is Christ and to die is gain.*

—Philippians 1:21

To my readers,

Well, we have come to the end of our journey. A continuous prayer resonates within my heart for all of you…

"Lord, please help those who read *Sold Out: Live for Jesus* experience a deeper, more intimate relationship with You. May any head knowledge gained through this little book be moved to heart knowledge so that change takes place from the inside out. I pray that each reader desires a relationship with Jesus twenty-four hours a day, seven days a week, resulting in a more Christ-centered and less self-centered life. Oh God, in the depths of their souls, help them listen to Your tender voice. Help them to be sensitive to the leading of the Holy Spirit. Please help each one change her thought life to a prayer life. Thank you for hearing these requests. I love you, God, my Father. In the name above all names, Your Son, Jesus. Amen."

As I close my laptop and recline in my prayer chair, a sense of relief captures my soul. Warmth consumes my heart. Praise fills the room. May the words from this book inspire, encourage, and spur you forward in developing a life sold out for Jesus.

From My Heart to Yours,

Carla McDougal
Founder of Reflective Life Ministries
Author of *Sold Out, My Prayer Chair,* and *Reflecting Him*

***

www.carlamcdougal.com
www.reflectivelifeministries.org

# IMAGE REFERENCES

Image 1 – Refresh Your Connections. Purchased.
http://www.istockphoto.com/photo/team-work-803575.

Image 2 – Pray 911 (10.17.2014).
http://www.freeimages.com/photo/1095705.

Image 3 – God Designs (10.17.2014).
http://www.freeimages.com/photo/716931.

Image 4 – Divine Assignments (10.17.2014).
http://www.freeimages.com/photo/498766.

Image 5 – God's Garden (10.11.2014).
http://www.freeimages.com/photo/460186. Fernando Fazzane. Sao Paulo, Brazil.

Image 6 – God Plans (10.29.2014). Reflective Life Ministries owns image.

Image 7 – Refuel Your Heart (3.6.2015).
http://www.freeimages.com/photo/1385767.

Image 8 – Forgiveness: Fresh Start. Carla McDougal owns this image.

Image 9 – Understanding: Never Forsaken (10.10.2014).
http://www.freeimages.com/browse.phtml?f=download&id=1388300.

Image 10 – Prayer: God's Ultimate Plan. Carla McDougal owns image.

Image 11 – God's Word: Scripture Hunt (10.16.2014).
http://www.freeimages.com/photo/1167176.

Image 12 – Praise: Thankful Attitude (10.11.2014).
http://www.freeimages.com/photo/1441782.

Image 13 – Restore Your Soul. Purchased.
http://www.istockphoto.com/photo/vintage-photo-of-woman-relaxing-at-the-lake-in-sunset-43138790.

Image 14 – Rest: The Heavens Declare. Carla McDougal owns this image.

Image 15 – Encouragement: God's Glory (3.6.2015). http://www.freeimages.com/browse.phtml?f=download&id =1445989.

Image 16 – Peace: Unexpected Storms (3.6.2015). http://www.freeimages.com/photo/323549.

Image 17 - Rescued: Under the Surface (10.17.2015). http://www.freeimages.com/photo/1439802.

Image 18 – Order: Discovering the Light (10.24.2014). http://www.freeimages.com/photo/1359067.

Image 19 – Renew Your Mind. Purchased. http://www.istockphoto.com/photo/personal-communication-33626040.

Image 20 – Abide: Love Deep (10.17.2014). http://www.freeimages.com/photo/1415366.

Image 21 – Surrender: Inside the Walls of Guilt (3.6.2015). http://www.freeimages.com/browse.phtml?f=download&id= 941739.

Image 22 – Release: Spiritual Junk Closets (10.17.2014). http://www.freeimages.com/photo/1329506.

Image 23 – Believe: God's Voice. Carla McDougal owns this image.

Image 24 – Laugh: God's Medicine. Purchased. http://www.istockphoto.com/photo/laughing-woman-on-compu ter-8077190.

Image 25 – Rebuild Your Strength. Purchased. http://www.istockphoto.com/photo/older-man-holding-a-bible-10002282.

Image 26 – Spiritual Life: Balancing Act. Carla McDougal owns this image.

Image 27 – Numbers: Cord of Three (10.16.2014). http://www.freeimages.com/photo/1162571.

Image 28 – Busyness: The Super-Hero Syndrome (10.12.2014) Purchased. http://www.istockphoto.com/photo/woman-opening-her-shirt-like-a-superhero-30824702.

Image 29 – Conversations: Fighting Fires (10.16.2014). http://www.freeimages.com/browse.phtml?f=search&txt=fires&w=1.

Image 30 – Families: To Mom, With Love. Carla McDougal owns this image.

Image 31 – Realign Your Attitude (3.6.2015). http://www.freeimages.com/photo/300092.

Image 32 – Transitions: Journey Through Changes (05.29.2015). Purchased. http://www.istockphoto.com/photo/changes-36611750.

Image 33 – Silence: A Hidden Message (3.6.2015). http://www.freebibleimages.org/photos/zechariah-john/.

Image 34 – Life: Short Cuts (05.29.2015). Purchased. http://www.istockphoto.com/photo/driving-to-olympos-11524912.

Image 35 – Choices: Decision Dilemma (05.29.2015). Purchased. http://www.istockphoto.com/photo/girl-finding-the-solution-32886700.

Image 36 – Unexpected: Blockades (3.6.2015). http://www.freeimages.com/photo/1159376.

Image 37 – Refill Your Hope. Carla McDougal owns this image.

Image 38 – Trust: A Room with a View. Carla McDougal owns this image.

Image 39 – The Cross: Redeemed (10.12.2014). http://www.freeimages.com/photo/1354974.

Image 40 – The Word: Spiritual Nourishment (10.13.2014). http://www.freeimages.com/photo/868023.

Image 41 – The Building Process: Living Stone (10.14.2014). Purchased. http://www.istockphoto.com/photo/the-open-tomb-of-jesus-in-jerusalem-35657716.

Image 42 – A Solid Rock: Precious Stones (10.14.2014).
http://www.freeimages.com/photo/872383.

Image 43 – Ready Your Walk (3.6.2015).
http://www.freeimages.com/photo/804489.

Image 44 – God's Purposes: Just for The Unjust (3.6.2015).
http://www.freeimages.com/photo/857370.

Image 45 – God's Ways: Marriage Bliss (10.14.2014).
http://www.freeimages.com/photo/592353.

Image 46 – God's Provisions: Ready? (3.6.2015).
http://www.freeimages.com/photo/834341.

Image 47 – God's Word: When God Speaks, Listen (10.12.2014).
http://www.freeimages.com/browse.phtml?f=search&w=1&txt=smile&p=7.

Image 48 – God's Care: Cast it All. Purchased.
http://www.istockphoto.com/photo/young-mother-overwhelmed-by-her-kids-36305654.

# ENDNOTES

1. Strong's Exhaustive Concordance: New American Standard Bible. 1995. Updated ed. La Habra: Lockman Foundation. http://www.blueletterbible.org/lang/lexicon/lexicon.cfm?Strongs=G2198&t=KJV.

2. Strong's Exhaustive Concordance: New American Standard Bible. 1995. Updated ed. La Habra: Lockman Foundation. http://www.blueletterbible.org/lang/lexicon/lexicon.cfm?Strongs=G2588&t=KJV.

3. Strong's Exhaustive Concordance: New American Standard Bible. 1995. Updated ed. La Habra: Lockman Foundation. http://www.blueletterbible.org/lang/lexicon/lexicon.cfm?Strongs=G5590&t=KJV.

4. Strong's Exhaustive Concordance: New American Standard Bible. 1995. Updated ed. La Habra: Lockman Foundation. http://www.blueletterbible.org/lang/lexicon/lexicon.cfm?Strongs=G1271&t=KJV.

5. Strong's Exhaustive Concordance: New American Standard Bible. 1995. Updated ed. La Habra: Lockman Foundation. http://www.blueletterbible.org/lang/lexicon/lexicon.cfm?Strongs=G26&t=KJV.

6. Strong's Exhaustive Concordance: New American Standard Bible. 1995. Updated ed. La Habra: Lockman Foundation. http://www.blueletterbible.org/lang/lexicon/lexicon.cfm?Strongs=G3306&t=KJV.

7. Strong's Exhaustive Concordance: New American Standard Bible. 1995. Updated ed. La Habra: Lockman Foundation. http://www.blueletterbible.org/lang/lexicon/lexicon.cfm?Strongs=G2479&t=KJV.

8. Strong's Exhaustive Concordance: New American Standard Bible. 1995. Updated ed. La Habra: Lockman Foundation. http://www.blueletterbible.org/lang/lexicon/lexicon.cfm?Strongs=G3598&t=KJV.

9. Strong's Exhaustive Concordance: New American Standard Bible. 1995. Updated ed. La Habra: Lockman Foundation. http://www.blueletterbible.org/lang/lexicon/lexicon.cfm?Strongs=G2117&t=KJV.

10. Strong's Exhaustive Concordance: New American Standard Bible. 1995. Updated ed. La Habra: Lockman Foundation. http://www.blueletterbible.org/lang/lexicon/lexicon.cfm?Strongs=G1680&t=KJV.

11. Strong's Exhaustive Concordance: New American Standard Bible. 1995. Updated ed. La Habra: Lockman Foundation. http://www.blueletterbible.org/lang/lexicon/lexicon.cfm?Strongs=G1680&t=KJV.

12. Strong's Exhaustive Concordance: New American Standard Bible. 1995. Updated ed. La Habra: Lockman Foundation. http://www.blueletterbible.org/lang/lexicon/lexicon.cfm?Strongs=G1971&t=KJV.

13. Strong's Exhaustive Concordance: New American Standard Bible. 1995. Updated ed. La Habra: Lockman Foundation. http://www.blueletterbible.org/lang/lexicon/lexicon.cfm?Strongs=G97&t=KJV.

14. Strong's Exhaustive Concordance: New American Standard Bible. 1995. Updated ed. La Habra: Lockman Foundation. http://www.blueletterbible.org/lang/lexicon/lexicon.cfm?Strongs=G1051&t=KJV.

15. Strong's Exhaustive Concordance: New American Standard Bible. 1995. Updated ed. La Habra: Lockman Foundation. http://www.blueletterbible.org/lang/lexicon/lexicon.cfm?Strongs=G4073&t=KJV.

16. Strong's Exhaustive Concordance: New American Standard Bible. 1995. Updated ed. La Habra: Lockman Foundation. http://www.blueletterbible.org/lang/lexicon/lexicon.cfm?Strongs=G3037&t=KJV.

17. Strong's Exhaustive Concordance: New American Standard Bible. 1995. Updated ed. La Habra: Lockman Foundation. http://www.blueletterbible.org/lang/lexicon/lexicon.cfm?Strongs=G2198&t=KJV.

18. Strong's Exhaustive Concordance: New American Standard Bible. 1995. Updated ed. La Habra: Lockman Foundation. http://www.blueletterbible.org/lang/lexicon/lexicon.cfm?Strongs=G3037&t=KJV.

19. Strong's Exhaustive Concordance: New American Standard Bible. 1995. Updated ed. La Habra: Lockman Foundation. http://www.blueletterbible.org/lang/lexicon/lexicon.cfm?Strongs=H3368&t=KJV.

20. Strong's Exhaustive Concordance: New American Standard Bible. 1995. Updated ed. La Habra: Lockman Foundation. http://www.blueletterbible.org/lang/Lexicon/Lexicon.cfm?strongs=G1137&t=KJV.

21. Strong's Exhaustive Concordance: New American Standard Bible. 1995. Updated ed. La Habra: Lockman Foundation. http://www.blueletterbible.org/lang/lexicon/lexicon.cfm?Strongs=G4043&t=KJV.

22. Strong's Exhaustive Concordance: New American Standard Bible. 1995. Updated ed. La Habra: Lockman Foundation. http://www.blueletterbible.org/lang/lexicon/lexicon.cfm?Strongs=G4043&t=KJV.

23. Strong's Exhaustive Concordance: New American Standard Bible. 1995. Updated ed. La Habra: Lockman Foundation. http://www.blueletterbible.org/lang/lexicon/lexicon.cfm?Strongs=G5293&t=KJV.

24. http://www.biblestudytools.com/lexicons/greek/nas/hupotasso.html.

25. Strong's Exhaustive Concordance: New American Standard Bible. 1995. Updated ed. La Habra: Lockman Foundation. http://www.blueletterbible.org/lang/lexicon/lexicon.cfm?Strongs=G1108&t=KJV.

# AUTHOR'S PREVIOUS BOOKS

MY PRAYER CHAIR NOW AVAILABLE IN ENGLISH, SPANISH, AND AUDIOBOOK

My Prayer Chair, winner of three book awards, is now available in three versions— English, Spanish, and Audio Book. How often do you communicate with Jesus? Every day or just in times of need? Do you view prayer as a privilege or a last resort? My Prayer Chair encourages the reader to engage in an ongoing conversation with God - 24/7. Free downloadable PDF Leader's Guides available at www.reflectivelifeministries.org

REFLECTING HIM BIBLE STUDY AND RIBBONS OF RAINBOWS

One of the most powerful teaching tools available for the whole family! Ribbons of Rainbows, the newest book offered by Reflective Life Ministries, tells the story of two young Stones in search of God's glory. Teach the same truths to your children as you learn through the Bible study Reflecting Him. Perfect for family devotionals, one-on-one conversations, and even used as homeschool curriculum. Reflecting Him offers a Leader's Guide, Teaching Video Series, the movie "Behind the Veil" with the same lessons embedded in the storyline, free promotional material, and more.